Tropical Fish

C.J. Harrison

John Bartholomew & Son Limited
Edinburgh and London

Contents

First published in Great Britain 1976 *by*
JOHN BARTHOLOMEW & SON LIMITED
12 Duncan Street, Edinburgh EH9 1TA
And at 216 High Street, Bromley BR1 1PW

ISBN 0 7028 1091 6

1st edition

Designed and illustrated by Allard Design Group Limited
Printed in Great Britain by W. S. Cowell Limited, Ipswich, Suffolk

Introduction

Despite the understandable enthusiasm that accompanies the decision to set up a tropical aquarium, the temptation to buy equipment impulsively must be resisted at all costs. A little forethought will avoid the expensive mistakes and disappointments that can sometimes mar an introduction to the fascinating world of tropical fishkeeping. The beginner should first decide a few basic matters: how much money can be spared to set up the tank? How much space is available? What types of fish are to be kept? Some items of equipment are quite unnecessary for the beginner, or at least their purchase can be put off for some months.

Fortunately the most expensive items are not automatically the most desirable for a first aquarium, where simplicity of operation should be the ideal. The money saved here should be put towards the real essentials: the largest aquarium, within reason, that you can afford and accommodate, reliable equipment, and healthy stock. Before finally committing yourself to a particular scheme, bear in mind not only the initial set-up that you are contemplating, but also how easily you will be able to expand the scope of your equipment to include, say, breeding, quarantining, and the keeping of types of fish with special requirements. In all these matters your local aquatic dealer can be an invaluable adviser.

There are basically two sets of classifications of fish that the hobbyist needs to concern himself with — coldwater or tropical, freshwater or marine. For the purpose of this book we are referring specifically to tropical freshwater fish, though it must be remembered that there is no hard-and-fast dividing line between each of the pairs: some species of fish commonly accepted as tropical will tolerate, after acclimatisation, a temperature lower than that at which many of the fancy varieties of goldfish are kept.

Similarly, one can find freshwater fish in the estuaries and tidal reaches of rivers where the water has a salt content almost as high as the open sea. The species covered in this book are basically those that will live happily in normal tropical freshwater aquarium conditions, and any deviation from this that they might prefer will be detailed in the individual description.

Why choose tropical fish?

We come across tropical aquaria so often that surely no one can be unaware of the great interest they often stimulate. Yet how many have been deterred from setting up their own tank by the apparent delicacy of the fish, or the seeming complexity of the equipment required? Yet these initial apprehensions are far, far removed from reality.

Almost everyone has kept a goldfish at some time, usually in a bowl — which is the worst possible setting for these fish. Unfortunately, it is the experiences here that tend to colour attitudes to all fishkeeping: the memory of this boring, and perhaps equally bored, creature swimming around in small circles, needing to be cleaned out each day, and then probably dying mysteriously after a few months. What could be more disappointing? Yet this is what people are likely to remember when tropical fish are mentioned, assuming that their 'exotic' nature will bring still more problems in caring for them. Nothing could be further from the truth! Almost all the equipment controlling their environment is automatic and trouble-free; those few items that are not will require just a minimum of periodic attention.

So, given that there are no difficulties in providing just the right conditions for tropical fish, let us consider in what way they are superior to coldwater fish. Their aesthetic appeal is obviously strong: tropical fish are found in almost every conceivable colour, and in a multitude of body shapes. Some are lively and boisterous, some are shy and secretive, and some are overwhelmingly possessive. In many fish the colours are vivid; in others the markings are more sombre, providing a form of camouflage to protect them from their natural enemies. Their body shapes and features will often prove a good indication of their habits or the conditions they encounter in the wild: the slender bodies of the fast-swimming rasboras, the sucker mouths of the loaches, enabling them to keep a firm hold to rocks and plants in fast-flowing streams, the small and tapered mouths of the botias, ideally suited for probing into the gravel in the search for food.

The second advantage over those coldwater species generally kept in indoor aquaria is on the point of size: many of the most popular tropical fish do not exceed $1\frac{1}{2}$-2 in. in length, and this means that far more fish can be kept in a given size of aquarium. This does not mean that those who happen to prefer large fish will be disappointed — far from it, for many of the more serious

aquarists keep specimens of 18 in. or more in length. But these are likely to demand aquaria of sizes far beyond the means, or desire, of the average beginner.

Thinking back again to one's early experiences with goldfish, the biggest mistake is likely to be the assumption that they will not grow much beyond the 2-3 in. size they were when purchased — and the tank will probably be stocked on that basis. In fact, provided conditions are favourable, they can reach double that size or even more. Gradual overcrowding caused by such growth will not be noticed during the cold months of the year, since the oxygen content of the water will be quite adequate for their needs, but with the first spell of hot weather they will all be gasping for air at the top of the aquarium : unless quick action is taken to correct the situation all the occupants could die within a few hours. Tropical fish can, and do, grow in the aquarium but we know fairly accurately the size they will eventually reach and can make allowance for this when first stocking the tank. Furthermore, since the ideal temperature of a tropical aquarium is similar to that found in an average room during a warm summer's day, there is not likely to be any sudden fall in the oxygen content of the water or increased oxygen requirement from the fish. The third advantage of tropical aquaria is in an area which is generally quite neglected by coldwater fishkeepers : that of plants. Not only are there hundreds of varieties suitable for aquatic cultivation but they will thrive and multiply provided their basic requirements are met. A few species of fich notably motynnic and como of tho largo cichlidc will devour the softer-leaved plants with relish, but care can be taken to prevent the two being present in the same aquarium.

Below, for easy summary, are listed some of the more common fallacies connected with tropical fishkeeping :
Tropical fish are not delicate 'hothouse' creatures — with the obvious exception of the temperature of their environment, their needs are much the same as those of our own native fish found in rivers and lakes.
The equipment is not dangerous — providing you do not fool about with it.
The equipment is not expensive to operate.
You do not have to clean out the tropical tank every week — if you have an efficient filter this is unnecessary, but the fish appreciate a partial change of water (about one quarter) every month or two.
Fish do not over-eat — and the food they do not eat can decay at the bottom of the aquarium and cause problems.

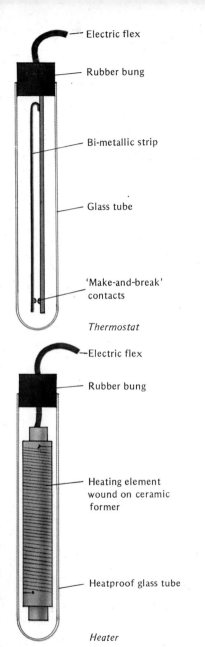

- Electric flex
- Rubber bung
- Bi-metallic strip
- Glass tube
- 'Make-and-break' contacts

Thermostat

As the water cools, the bi-metallic strip bends to close the gap between the two contacts, and this restores the flow of current to the heater: in due course the water warms up, the strip reacts to the change in temperature and the current flow stops as the contacts spring apart. Most models have a small magnet to ensure a crisp opening and closing of the contacts.

- Electric flex
- Rubber bung
- Heating element wound on ceramic former
- Heatproof glass tube

Heater

The heater is usually a glass test-tube around 6 in. long, containing a heating element wound onto a ceramic core: the open end is made watertight with a rubber bung, through which passes a length of electric flex.

Heating

The majority of tropical fish can tolerate a temperature anywhere in the range of 20-30 °C. and often even higher or lower than this depending on the conditions found in their native areas. They can also tolerate a considerable fluctuation in temperature — at least 3 °C. providing it occurs gradually over a period of an hour or two, but they do not like any sudden changes such as they might experience when being tipped straight from one aquarium into another. Generally they will be happiest if kept at around 24 °C., and with a fairly small fluctuation — perhaps 1 or 2 degrees.

Occasionally you will encounter a species that does prefer the aquarium a few degrees warmer or cooler, or you might wish to encourage spawning by raising the temperature to around 27 °C. for a few days: these possibilities are covered in the relevant chapter and need not concern the novice at this stage. If the aquarium is kept permanently at a level well outside the ideal for the particular species, one of two things will happen: if it is kept too warm, the fish will tend to be livelier and perhaps a little more brightly coloured, but will live for perhaps no more than half the expected time: if kept too cool, the fish will be less active, less colourful, much slower in their growth rate and more often prone to illness.

The most popular form of aquarium heating in use nowadays — and it is also about the cheapest and most reliable — is electricity: the necessary equipment comprises a heater, thermostat, and thermometer.

There are some variations in style of heater, some having much longer and narrower glass tubes, others being encased in a long flexible plastic pipe, which, unlike other types, must be buried just beneath the surface of the gravel. Those heaters employing glass tubes should be laid horizontally on the surface of the gravel or, ideally, fixed with a clip just ½ in. above it, preferably near the back of the tank where a suitable rock or thicket of plants will provide good camouflage. Heaters should never be removed from the aquarium while plugged into the mains: they become extremely hot and might explode with such treatment.

The simplest type of thermostat uses a similar glass tube and rubber bung, and contains a bi-metallic strip which controls the flow of current between two electrical contacts. The thermostat is placed upright in the aquarium, preferably in a corner, so that the water level comes between ½ in. and 1½ in. from the top of the tube. These thermostats are usually pre-set at the factory to provide a temperature in the range of 24-25 °C., but the setting can be adjusted if desired by unplugging the unit from the mains, carefully removing the glass tube, and fractionally turning the small screw that tensions the bi-metallic strip. Although this is very much a trial-and-error method, with a little practice accurate results can be achieved.

In addition to cheapness, this design has the further advantage of being tamper-proof in households where young children are present. More elaborate models may incorporate a small knob on the top of the instrument which adjusts the temperature setting with a minimum of fuss : others, known as 'external' thermostats, are clipped onto the outside of the tank and sense the temperature of the water through the aquarium glass. With this latter type, the spring fixing clip must hold the baseplate on the thermostat in firm and perfect contact with the glass, otherwise accuracy of control will not be possible.

The last item — the thermometer — is available in numerous designs, but for accuracy a mercury-filled one is best : for legibility, however, small circular dial-type thermometers are now very popular. Whatever the model you choose, try to keep it in a position (ideally in one corner at the front of the tank) where it can be easily observed, almost automatically, each time you pass the tank.

Heaters are available in a number of ratings, from 25-200 watts and the choice will depend on the size of the aquarium ; a check should also be made that the heaters do not exceed the maximum loading of the thermostat you plan to use — your dealer can probably advise you on this if there is no recommendation by the manufacturer.

It should be remembered that money is not saved by using heaters of a wattage well below the recommended level : it just means that they take longer to heat the water before the thermostat switches off. Heaters far in excess of the recommended wattage may heat the water of a small tank so quickly that the fish do not have as much time as they might like to adjust to the change.

The correct size of heater is essential, and in larger aquaria this may mean the use of two, or more, heaters to achieve the necessary total wattage : this also gives an extra margin of safety should one of them fail unexpectedly. The recommendations for the more popular sizes of aquaria are as follows :

18 in. x 10 in. x 10 in. = 100 watts
24 in. x 15 in. x 12 in. = 150 watts (or 2 x 75 watts)

36 in. x 15 in. x 12 in. = 2 x 135 watts
48 in. x 15 in. x 12 in. = 2 x 150 watts

For small breeding or quarantine tanks, heaters of 40 or 60 watts should be suitable.

Periodically the heating circuit should be unplugged from the mains supply, allowed to cool down for ten minutes and the equipment carefully removed from the tank. The contacts of the thermostat should be examined for any signs of 'arcing', indicated by severe pitting or a surround of black soot. If this is present, the unit is likely to fail and should be replaced immediately. The heater should be examined for signs of condensation or blackened patches inside the tube; again, these forewarn of trouble and the unit should be replaced. If the circuit employs more than one heater, the whole should be plugged into the mains for just five seconds, then unplugged and each of the heaters felt in turn to ensure that it has become slightly warm and so is still working properly: occasionally heaters do fail without any apparent signs. If all is well, everything can be replaced in the aquarium.

Should the glass tube of the thermostat be accidentally broken a new one can be obtained and easily fitted: this is not possible with the heater, however, since this instrument is specially sealed in manufacture to prevent any dampness corroding the element.

One item of equipment I have not yet mentioned is the combined heater/thermostat, a rather larger glass tube incorporating the heater at the lower end and the thermostat in the upper half. This item is particularly popular in the United States, but does have a couple of disadvantages: if either part of the unit develops a fault the whole has to be discarded, it is usually available in only a limited range of wattages, and since it cannot be connected to additional heaters it is not really suited to large sizes of aquaria.

Let us now look a little more carefully at the safety aspects of fishkeeping from an electrical point of view.

The thermostat will have to be connected to the heater(s), and since there are so many designs you ought to follow the manufacturer's instructions carefully. If you are using more than one heater, the correct procedure is to take from each heater one wire, bared for $\frac{1}{2}$ in., and twist them together; the remaining wires should be similarly treated. You then treat each of the two 'bunches' of wires as you would the individual wires of a single heater when connecting to the 'stat. All electrical connexions should be made with the proper insulated screw connecting blocks — quite cheap and virtually fool-proof — and then covered with several wrappings of plastic insulation tape.

All these joints should be placed — and fixed if necessary — in such a position that they cannot possibly fall into the water. If you buy or make a good distribution panel, with sockets and switches for the various electrical items, you will find it one of the best investments ever made. Next we come to the question of whether or not to earth the aquarium and fittings : there are such differing opinions on this matter that it is very much up to the individual. Expert advice should be taken from a qualified electrician if in doubt.

Now the unspoken worry of many hobbyists — power cuts and failures. These often cause quite unnecessary panic and fear among many fishkeepers. Providing prompt action is taken — and the larger the tank the less its occupants will suffer — there is no need to worry at the prospect of being without heat for four or five hours on even the coldest of nights. In the event of power failure, and after ensuring the switch controlling the lights in the cover is in the 'off' position, cover the tank all round with several thicknesses of newspaper and then drape a rug or blanket over this : if the room temperature can be raised to the region of 10 °C. or more by an independent means, so much the better. When the power is restored, just remove the wrappings and let the heater warm the water gradually. Whatever you do, don't pour hot water in to speed things up.

Finally, one useful tip. If you want to reduce heat loss from the aquarium and save on your electricity bills, cut panels of $\frac{1}{2}$ in. expanded polystyrene to cover the back and ends of the aquarium and stick or wedge them in place. Perhaps you are artistically inclined ; if so the back panel can be coloured to provide an attractive backdrop for the rocks and plants in the tank — but avoid the temptation to paint the plants on this panel.

Lighting

Light, as we perceive it, is of a single colour, but in reality that colour is composed of various proportions of each of the colours in the spectrum — and this is even the case with 'pure' white light. Not all these colours can be fully utilized by plants for the process of photosynthesis (on which they are dependent for their survival), so we have to ensure that the light source we choose is not seriously deficient in any of those essential colours. Sunlight, having its composition broadly across the spectrum, is very suitable; so are the normal clear tungsten light bulbs used in every home, though certainly not the coloured types used for decorative lighting effects; and some types of fluorescent tubes are also suitable, notably 'warm white', together with those specially developed for horticultural use.

As we have established, the sun provides us with a suitable type of light for aquatic plants: this fact is obvious to anyone who has studied the ponds and lakes in his neighbourhood. But, while it has a more than adequate intensity and duration — in the summer at least — daylight falls short of our requirements in terms of its lack of controllability and the fact that it will generally fall only onto the back or front glass panels rather than being directly overhead. This causes plants on the side of the aquarium nearest to the sun to grow in profusion, thus masking the remainder.

We therefore have to rely to a large extent on artificial lighting for the success of the plants, and for the beginner ordinary light bulbs have the advantages of being inexpensive and simple to install, suitable for almost any size of aquarium (by selecting the appropriate number and wattage of bulbs used), and they give the aquarium a pleasant tone and attractive appearance. Different plants will be found to have slightly differing light requirements, but, as a general guide, aquaria of 12 in. or 15 in. depth of water will require 40 watts of lighting per foot of length for an average of around ten hours each day. This can be modified to suit a particular situation, but you should avoid excessively long or short periods of lighting, since this will not give the best results with the plants. You should also avoid using bulbs of more than 60 watts, since they become excessively hot: this can lead to an overheated water-surface which may harm the fish.

Fluorescent tubes have become increasingly popular in recent years despite the considerable cost of the control unit, their main advantages being both the high intensity of light they produce

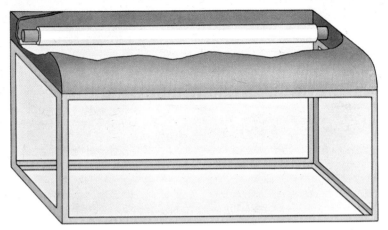

Fluorescent lighting: an increasingly popular method of lighting the aquarium

Photosynthesis: too little or too much light can easily have an adverse effect on the plants, and as a corollary the fish must suffer.

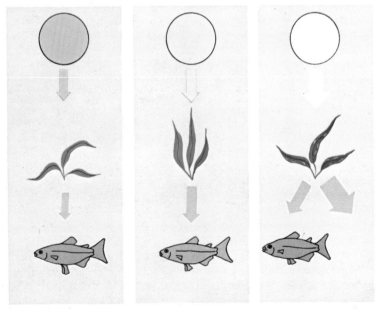

relative to their consumption of electricity, and the fact that they remain far cooler in operation than bulbs. Their intensity of light is such that, in order to calculate the wattage required for a given size tank, one should take one quarter of the figure mentioned earlier for ordinary tungsten bulbs : this means, for example, using a 15 or 20 watt tube for a tank 24 in. long, for an average of ten hours each day. Their cool-running qualities make them ideal for very deep aquaria of 18 in. and more, where a considerable intensity of light is needed to reach the plants effectively. In addition to the 'warm white' tube previously recommended, horticultural tubes developed specially for new plants are now available, of which Gro-Lux is an internationally known brand name. These give off a rather pinkish hue — under which the orange- and red-coloured fish acquire an exceptional (even unnatural) fluorescent brilliance. If you do settle for these special tubes, you must remember that they have only one half of the light output of ordinary fluorescent tubes.

The beginner should not worry about sticking too rigidly to the various formulae for estimating the lighting requirements of aquatic plants, there is a certain degree of latitude in the matter. More important by far is that he should be able to recognise from the appearance of the plants themselves whether or not he is meeting their needs. If the plants are slow to grow and settle down, turn a paler shade of green or even yellow, and look generally drab and listless, they are almost certainly not receiving sufficient light. If the plant leaves, the rocks, and even the glass panels of the aquarium get covered in algae, either as a solid green mass or of the thread-like variety, then there is too much illumination. Providing the aquarium is sited in a reasonably bright room — though there should be little or no sunlight falling directly onto it — the plants will need no artificial light during the course of a week or two's holiday, assuming they are well established and healthy before-hand : they will then regain their former growth rate within a few days of your return.

If the aquarium is situated in a dark position, a fortnight without any light at all could be serious : in this instance, if a friend is unable to help by switching on the light for a few hours each day, you might consider the use of a time switch. Under no circumstances should you leave the lights on for the whole of your absence, even with bulbs of a lower wattage than usual.

The foregoing paragraphs have been written, almost without exception, from the standpoint of the plants — for it is they, and not the fish, that find adequate lighting so indispensable.

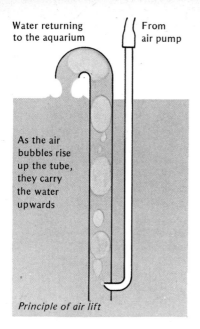

Water returning to the aquarium

From air pump

As the air bubbles rise up the tube, they carry the water upwards

Principle of air lift

When the air-lift is operating, a vacuum is created under the plate and this gently sucks water through the layer of gravel and the perforations and into the cavity beneath the plate, from where it is returned to the aquarium via the air-lift.

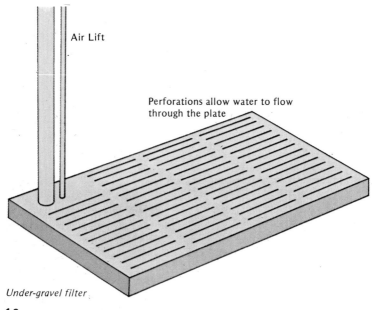

Air Lift

Perforations allow water to flow through the plate

Under-gravel filter

Aeration and filtration

In the same way that our own environment can become polluted, so also can that of the fish. Nature generally copes perfectly well with rectifying this state in the wild: it does this either by providing a continuous supply of fresh water, as is the case with rivers, or by purifying a static body of water — such as lakes and ponds — by the action of bacteria. Those particular bacteria thrive wherever there is a plentiful supply of oxygen in the water, which there must be for the fish to survive, and they convert unsightly solid waste matter into water-soluble chemical products which, in moderation at least, are quite harmless to the fish.

In turn, certain of these chemical products — nitrates in particular — are essential for the growth of aquatic plants. In this way the aquatic environment can be largely 'self-cleansing', given three factors: a large area of water surface for maximum oxygen absorption; a reasonable level of aquatic plant life; and a fairly low concentration of fish with the resultant minimum of excreta. Since the average home aquarium will fall short on at least one, and probably all three, of these criteria, we are left with a choice: either meet the criteria half-way and use suitable equipment to help nature do the work more efficiently than it does in the wild, or, alternatively, employ mechanical filtration methods.

Biological Filtration

Although the valuable aerobic bacteria exist in only quite low concentrations in free water, they can form dense colonies if provided with a 'home' on which they can become established without disturbance: these colonies appear as a jelly-like film, just a fraction of an inch thick, that gives a slimy coating to aquarium ornaments, thermostat tubes, and the like. They also form in the topmost layer of the aquarium gravel, where the oxygen-rich water permeates sufficiently to keep them alive: but deeper down in the gravel bed they cannot normally survive in quantity since there is insufficient oxygen. However, in the process known as biological (or under-gravel) filtration we utilize the full depth of gravel as a 'home' for these bacterial colonies by causing the water to flow steadily and continuously through it. This means it can support a heavy concentration of bacteria, which in turn means that it has the capability of breaking down very considerable quantities of waste matter in the aquarium.

We can achieve a suitable flow of water in the aquarium by

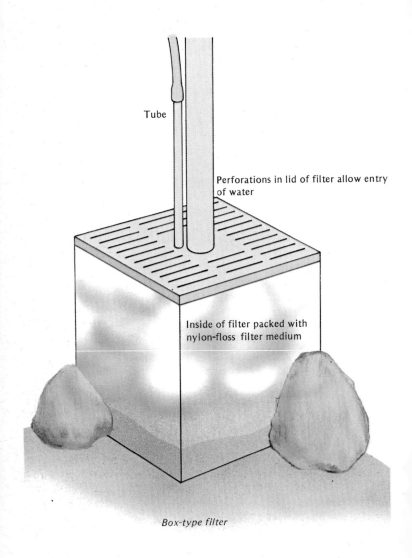

Tube

Perforations in lid of filter allow entry of water

Inside of filter packed with nylon-floss filter medium

Box-type filter

placing immediately under the gravel one or more perforated plastic plates, each equipped with an air-lift so as to cover most of the aquarium base. When the air-lift is operating, a vacuum is created under the plate and this gently sucks water through the layer of gravel and the perforations and into the cavity beneath the plate, from where it is returned to the aquarium via the air-lift. An alternative system uses a grid of perforated plastic tubes to cover the base of the aquarium, but in all other respects is identical.

The success of biological filtration is dependant on a depth of gravel sufficient for the colonies to establish themselves, and on it being a suitable grade: the absolute minimum depth of gravel should be 1 in., though double this would be better, and a grade of 1/8 in. or 3/16 in. will allow an adequate flow of water. Very fine gravel or silver sand, however attractive it might look, is quite useless for biological filtration and has, in any context, a limited range of uses in the aquarium. This type of filtration must be operated continuously otherwise the bacteria will die, entailing a wait of perhaps ten days while they re-establish themselves.

There is obviously a limit to the quantity of waste matter that a biological filtration system can successfully process; as a guide, satisfactory results will be achieved if the aquarium is not stocked with fish beyond about two-thirds of its maximum capacity, and if they are not fed too heavily. Since the chemical products that result will be far in excess of what can be utilized by the plants, it is advisable to change about a quarter of the water every month or two to prevent an excessive concentration being formed.

Mechanical Filtration

This method involves passing the water through a suitable filter medium, such as nylon 'floss', which traps the solid waste matter and other rubbish in the aquarium. Periodically this floss will have to be removed from the filter and either rinsed out or renewed: this should be done at least once a week — more often if necessary — otherwise colonies of bacteria will form on the surface of the filter medium and greatly restrict the flow of water. This process cannot remove any dissolved impurities in the aquarium water, but normally these will be quite satisfactorily dealt with by the aerobic bacteria found in any body of water, and by the normal exchange of gases between the water and the aquarium — aided by aeration if possible.

It is possible to use a special carbon or charcoal as an additional filter medium to carry out this filtration rôle, but since there is no

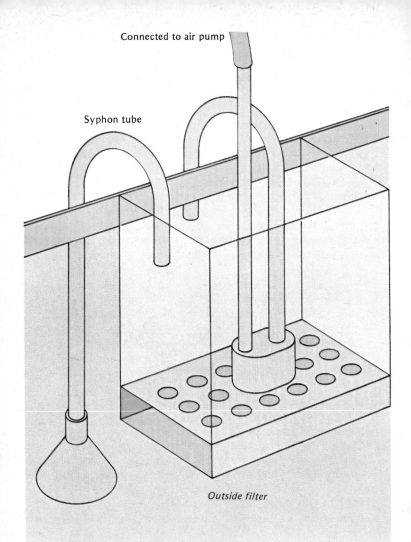

Connected to air pump

Syphon tube

Outside filter

simple way of telling when the carbon has exhausted its capacity to absorb these impurities, the hobbyist would do well not to rely too heavily on it.

If an outside filter is being used the only visible sign in the aquarium will usually be one, or possibly two, syphon tubes — each about $\frac{1}{2}$ in. in diameter — which carry aquarium water to the filter box for it to be cleaned and returned ; this type is therefore ideal for displays, but those models without their own power will need a fairly large quantity of air to operate at maximum efficiency. As with biological filtration, the fish will greatly appreciate a periodic partial change of water.

Aeration
This term covers all artificial methods of increasing the oxygen content of the water above the level achieved by normal absorption from the atmosphere at the water surface. To the aquarist it will usually mean more specifically the use of an air stone, otherwise known as a diffuser block, to break up the supply of air in the aquarium into a mist of fine bubbles, though a similar result is achieved by an air-operated filter.

Let us first establish one essential rule : never use aeration as a means of crowding more fish into an aquarium than would other-wise be permitted — except possibly as the most temporary expedient in an emergency. Not only would a failure of the air supply lead to the very quick death of all the fish — perhaps in just a few minutes, certainly before the trouble could be spotted — but such overcrowding will only result in stunted growth and un-healthy fish that can never be a credit to their owner. But in some senses aeration can be an extremely valuable asset to the hobbyist : by increasing the oxygen content in an uncrowded aquarium it will encourage the multiplication of the valuable aerobic bacteria in the water, thus in an aquarium with a very low concentration of fish, aeration alone may be sufficient to keep it crystal clear, without the need for additional filtration.

Another valuable point is the circulation of water encouraged by aeration : this distributes the surface water — which is most highly charged with oxygen, and is often quite hot from the light bulbs — around the whole tank, helping to keep conditions more even.

Air Pumps
Air pumps, also known as aerators, produce the air needed to operate filters, air stones, and the numerous plastic novelties

which some people insist on introducing into an otherwise natural-looking display. Their output, in terms of volume and pressure, is quite small, but even the cheapest is likely to operate one outside filter, or three internal filters or airstones, quite adequately. Most of the popular models incorporate a rubber diaphragm which pumps the air through a series of one-way valves set in a chamber: power comes from an electric coil which causes vibration of the arm on which the diaphragm is mounted. This type of air pump will meet the needs of most hobbyists — the larger models will operate 10 or 15 air stones, and use very little electricity.

Periodically the air filter in the pump — if one is fitted — should be closed, and if the output begins to fall the valve seatings should have the accumulated dirt and grime carefully removed with a pointed matchstick. The rubber diaphragm will normally need replacement every year or two, but this is a simple job.

Air Distribution

To convey the air from the pump to the aquarium we use flexible transparent plastic tubing with an outside diameter of approximately $\frac{1}{4}$ in. If more than one item of equipment is required to operate from the one pump it is necessary to split up the air to meet the needs, in terms of volume and pressure, of the various filters and air stones. This is done most easily with a series of airline valves, usually made of plastic but sometimes found in metal: with a little practice you will soon be able to achieve a steady flow of air to supply each item, though you may have to make minor adjustments each week to retain this balance. It is still possible to obtain T-pieces and clamps, a method of air control popular until a few years ago when rubber tubing was the only sort of airline available, but which requires very frequent adjustment to be satisfactory.

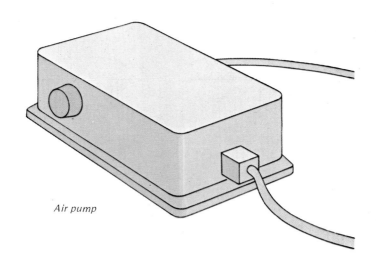

Air pump

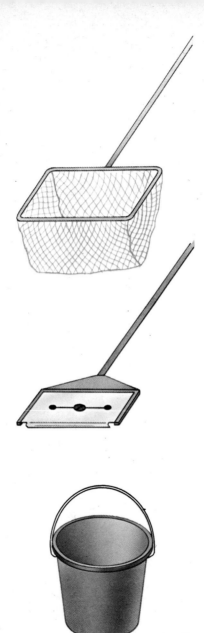

Net, scraper, and bucket

Miscellaneous equipment

A number of small items of equipment will be required for routine tasks in servicing the aquarium and ensuring the well-being of its occupants.

Nets

These are essential, in a suitable size and mesh, to catch the fish quickly, and to avoid uprooting the plants. Ideally, three are needed : two — say approximately 6 in. x 5 in. and 5 in. x 4 in. with a coarse mesh to catch the adult fish — and a smaller one in a very fine mesh to net very young fish and to catch live foods such as daphnia. Rather than chase the fish all round the aquarium, the nets should be used in pairs — one to drive the fish into the other. Special nets may be needed for exceptionally large aquaria or for fish exceeding about 5 in. in length.

Scrapers

The inside of the aquarium glass is likely to get covered with a fine coating of algae quite quickly, marring the display : by using a scraper on the glass each week, the occupants may be viewed as clearly as ever. Some scrapers incorporate a razor blade, and are very effective : this type is not recommended for use on aquaria constructed with silicone rubber sealant, since the blade can easily damage the seal. For these, use one of the many designs of plastic-faced scrapers.

Plastic Buckets

You will need to carry water to and from the aquarium, wash the gravel, examine newly purchased plants, and even find a home for the fish while the aquarium is being cleaned out. For all these purposes — and many more besides — a pair, or more, of two-gallon plastic buckets is essential. They should never be used for anything other than aquatic items.

Syphon Tube

A 6 ft. length of $\frac{1}{2}$ in. plastic tubing, preferably transparent, is needed to transfer water to and from the aquarium, and also for syphoning excess sediment and dead leaves from the bottom of the tank if no form of filtration is being used. If a short piece of more rigid plastic tubing, about 12 in. long, can be fitted onto one end, it will give easier and more accurate directional control.

The final item, one which will ensure the continued popularity of the aquarium in your household, is a large sheet of plastic.

Rocks and gravel

Rocks and gravel form an integral part of almost every furnished aquarium. The rocks make an attractive background to complement the bright colours of the plants, break up the flatness of the floor of the aquarium, and — for those fish whose nature it is to eat or dig up the aquatic plants — provide hiding places. The gravel will, at the very least, be a means of stopping reflection from the bare glass base of the tank, which most fish dislike intensely, but it is more commonly used as a medium in which the plants can take root and establish themselves.

Since the rockwork and gravel between them represent such a considerable mass in the aquarium, care should be taken to ensure that they are completely inert, or very nearly so, otherwise conditions will quickly become quite unsuitable for the fish. The worst offenders in this respect are chalk, marble, and spar which will dissolve and greatly harden the water; along with these we must also include cement and concrete which, unless several years old and well weathered, can prove equally disastrous. Materials particularly suitable include Westmorland stone, granite, flint, slate, and even well-washed coal. The author's particular favourite is sandstone, a fairly soft rock found in a wide range of hues — ranging from off-white through orange and brown to a pale violet — and in the most interesting shapes imaginable; in due course the surface of this rock will become covered with a thin coating of green algae, imparting an air of permanence to the display.

Gravel is a far more standardised item than the rockwork, though in recent years the unnatural, brightly coloured types have achieved a certain degree of popularity: about these, all that can be said is that if you happen to like the effect they create — use them. It will probably be found that the ordinary gravel, usually a mixture of fine pebbles of varied pale colours, provides a much better setting to show off the fish and plants to their best advantage. It comes in a range of grades, varying from 1/16 in. to $\frac{1}{4}$ in.; anything much finer, approaching sand in its consistency, is unlikely to achieve a permanently attractive display for a number of reasons, and anything larger can cause problems by trapping uneaten food particles which will then decay. The choice may perhaps be made on the basis of the size of aquarium and the size of the fish to be kept — thereby retaining some degree of relationship between the various component parts of the furnished aquarium. This pebble type of gravel tends to be very slightly soluble in soft water, though this process soon slows right down at a point well within the hardness limit tolerated by most fish. An alternative type of gravel is sometimes available, comprising small pieces of crushed rock; this is usually quite inert in water and advertised as such. The disadvantage with this is that the sharp edges will rapidly damage the mouths of those fish that forage in the gravel for their food, and whiskerless catfish are frequently seen as witness of its thoughtless use.

Some hobbyists still persist with the notion that, for successful plant growth, a layer of soil or peat is essential under the gravel. This is not so: the fish themselves will quickly provide all the nourishment the plants need — and more besides. In fact, such a layer of soil can create enormous problems of pollution.

Whenever there is the slightest doubt about the safety of any item to be included in the aquarium, it should first be tested. Quite simply find a clean glass bowl large enough to accommodate the item, fill it up with water almost to the top, and then introduce a few aquatic crustacea, such as daphnia or cyclops (*see section on live foods*). If they are still alive at the end of two weeks, you can be reasonably certain that the item will be equally harmless to fish.

Rock layout

Water

Water chemistry is an area to which a whole book could be devoted, yet the average hobbyist is well advised to leave the subject completely alone once he has understood the few basic rules that apply to fishkeeping. Only distilled water can be completely pure: all other sources will provide water which contains various proportions of dissolved gases, minerals, or other chemicals. This can be of vital importance in two particular respects: the first concerns the hardness of the water, the second its acidity or alkalinity.

Before rainwater finds its way into rivers or our water-supply systems, it will pass through various layers in the earth: some of these will contain materials that are highly soluble in water, such as chalk, whilst others will be less so, or totally insoluble. The amount of these dissolved solids can be measured, and this is usually expressed in terms of parts per million, abbreviated to p.p.m.

Water is commonly classified according to the following scale:

Soft	less than 50 p.p.m.
Moderately soft	50—100 p.p.m.
Slightly hard	100—150 p.p.m.
Moderately hard	150—250 p.p.m.
Hard	250—350 p.p.m.
Very hard	over 350 p.p.m.

Water supplies to cities will often be found to fall within the moderately hard category, though there can be considerable variation from this depending upon the source.

Most fishes can tolerate water between nil p.p.m. and well in excess of 500 p.p.m., but they will not stand for sudden or excessive changes in hardness: this affects the delicate mechanism of their body, and commonly results in a speedy death. Some hobbyists do, in fact, decide to keep particular species in water of a very low hardness — where this is the state they are used to in the wild — or else do so temporarily in an attempt to induce the spawning of some of the more difficult types. The average hobbyist is unlikely to encounter either of these situations, which demand the greatest of care if they are to be worthwhile, and so is far better advised to accept the water conditions as he finds them in his area.

If it is for some reason imperative to find a source of soft water, there are two inexpensive methods: rainwater, providing it is collected in containers free from any contamination, can be mixed with tap-water — though rainwater gathered after a lengthy dry period can contain large quantities of impurities from the atmosphere. Alternatively, the hardness of ordinary tap-water can be reduced by placing it in a clean pan or kettle and bringing it to boiling-point: the hardness that this method removes is known as 'temporary hardness', and is seen as the stone-like layer on the inside of kettles. The remaining hardness is known as the 'permanent hardness'.

Domestic water softeners are of no value to the aquarist, since they do not reduce the overall level of dissolved salts. It is possible, though, to purchase special ion-exchange resins which will effectively soften water; it is an expensive procedure if any quantity is to be treated. Thus it can be seen that it will be best to keep those species of fish that are known to be happy in water just as it comes from your tap — that, after all, is what your aquatic supplier uses for 99 per cent of his stock.

Acidity or alkalinity is generally expressed in terms of the pH scale, ranging from 0 to 14: 7.0 indicates neutral reaction, a value below this indicates acidity, above this alkalinity. Fish generally prefer the water to be fairly close to neutral — say, within the range 6.5–7.5 — and fortunately this state will generally be maintained indefinitely in an aquarium that has been set up and serviced with care. In the unlikely event of there being a considerable variation from this, and the fish showing signs of being affected by it, then the cause must be traced and removed: it may be a piece of rock or bark that was selected without sufficient caution. A partial change of water, perhaps one quarter, every twelve hours will probably restore the position to normal within a few days: this is a far better practice than adding chemicals to achieve a neutrality, for fish will not tolerate sudden changes in pH any more than those in hardness.

To summarise: ordinary tap-water will be perfectly suitable in almost every case, the only caution being with regard to chlorine and other dissolved gases it might contain. When setting up an aquarium for the first time, use cold water and let the heater bring it up to the correct temperature overnight: those few hours will rid the water of these gases, particularly if aided by aeration, and will also ensure the heating system is working properly before the fish are introduced.

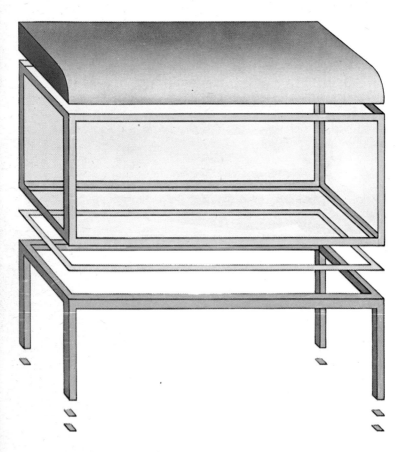

Setting up a tank

Siting and setting up the tank

As with any item of furniture, the aquarium must fit in with its surroundings if it is to be fully appreciated, and some thought should be given to its size, style, and location.

Size is a factor that is likely to be determined by financial, rather than aesthetic, considerations: it is sufficient to say that within reason, the larger the aquarium you select, the greater your chances of achieving an attractive and lasting display. In some countries aquaria are classified according to their dimensions — while elsewhere they are referred to on the basis of their capacity. Aquaria smaller than 18 in. x 12 in. x 12 in. have rather limited value from the display point of view, and are more likely to be used for quarantining or breeding purposes — holding a relatively low number of fish, and probably with few plants.

An ideal size for the beginner would be 24 in. x 15 in. x 12 in., the 15 in. height allowing for a more attractive presentation of the aquatic plants than the 12 in. tanks popular until a few years ago. If space permits, a larger size might be chosen — say a 36 in. x 15 in. x 12 in. or 48 in. x 15 in. x 12 in. — though the author feels that with these lengths an extra 3 in. on the width is essential if any 'depth' is to be achieved in the finished display: this is because refraction makes the distance from front to back of the aquarium appear much less than it really is.

There are many types of aquarium to choose from, and great advances have been made over the last decade in their appearance and water-tightness. Pressed steel or angle-iron framed aquaria, with the glass panels set in a bed of putty, are still popular — if only for their cheapness — but retain their long-term disadvantages of rusting and a tendency to leak when emptied and refilled. Some manufacturers have overcome the first problem by coating the frame with a thin layer of plastic material which, unless damaged, protects it from corrosion and gives it an attractive surface finish. Aquaria made entirely of plastic or perspex have been with us for many years — mainly in the smaller sizes — but while they have some advantages, their viewing panels may become covered in minute scratches after a time — thus giving a rather clouded appearance to the display.

The most important advances ever made in aquarium design are due to one product — silicone rubber sealant — which is an adhesive having an enormous bonding strength to glass, while permanently retaining its flexible, jelly-like texture. By using this

Washing gravel

The easiest way is to wash about 7 lb. at a time in a clean bucket under a running tap, stirring it up with your hand the whole time.

product, glass panels can be glued together to form a strong, completely watertight, frameless cube: aquaria of this style are now extremely popular, and a refinement is the addition of an attractive aluminium or plastic framework within which the aquarium is constructed. Such a framework imparts little strength in itself but is used more for ornamentation.

Whatever design of aquarium you choose, you will also need a matching cover to house the lighting and to minimise the loss of water through evaporation, which would otherwise be considerable. If the extra expense is a problem, a sheet of glass may be laid across the top, or held in place with special cover-glass clips, and a reflector placed on top of this: this would not really be recommended as a permanent measure since the plants will not do so well with this arrangement. Only a very small gap beneath the aquarium cover is needed to permit air to reach the water surface, anything excessive will not only encourage evaporation but also allow dust and dirt to get in and — even more important — the livelier types of fish to jump out.

You will now have to find something to support your aquarium; the support must be sufficiently strong to cope with its very considerable weight, high enough above the floor to put it in a

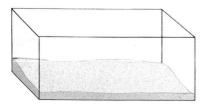

The gravel is then smoothed out, giving it a slightly greater depth at the back than at the front.

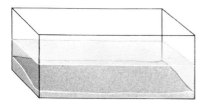

Now add cold water, trying not to disturb the gravel too much, until the aquarium is a little over half full.

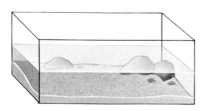

Next come the rocks, after a good wash and soak in clean, hot water, and their arrangement may take some time before the best effect is achieved.

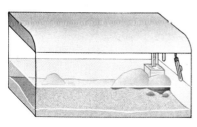

The heater and thermostat should be fixed in position, the filter installed and connected to the air pump, the aquarium cover fitted, and all the electrical items wired up ready to be switched on.

A little more water is added to bring the level up to 2 in. from the top of the aquarium: the remaining gap is to allow for the water that comes with the fish when you purchase them.

After ensuring that all the electrical connexions are free from splashes, no wires are dangling in the water, you may switch on.

comfortable viewing position, yet not too obtrusive. Angle-iron stands with welded joints are readily available in a wide range of sizes, and usually have a shelf for a second tank — for breeding or quarantine, perhaps — closer to the floor : a much better idea, surely, than putting too much faith in the top of a convenient cabinet, or in a shelf fixed to the wall.

Having purchased the necessary items, the time has come to make a start on the setting up. A position for the aquarium should be selected which ideally is bright but has little or no sun falling directly onto it : an excess of sunlight brings with it an excess of algae growing on the glass panels and plant leaves. The stand should be placed on small squares of hardboard or plywood to prevent the feet damaging the floor surface and if necessary a little extra packing added at one end until the tank is quite firm and level : this latter point should be checked out with a spirit level. Cut an expanded polystyrene ceiling tile into strips 1 in. wide, and use these as cushions all the way around between the top of the stand and the bottom of the aquarium.

The gravel should now be washed thoroughly, and you will need about 14 lb. of it per square foot of aquarium base to give a reasonable depth. It can then be tipped into the aquarium, the biological filter (if one is to be used) having previously been positioned on the base of the aquarium. After ensuring that all the electrical connexions are free from splashes, and no wires are dangling in the water, you may switch on.

By warming up the water from cold in this way, the correct working of the various items can be ensured — such as the temperature setting of the thermostat — and adjustment made if necessary. This procedure is always advisable when setting up a new aquarium : it avoids endangering the lives of valuable fish with untried equipment ; it also allows time for any dissolved gases the fresh water might contain to be released harmlessly into the atmosphere.

Providing the aquarium has been working satisfactorily for at least twenty-four hours, we may consider it safe to introduce the aquatic plants and a small selection of fish to their new environment. The plants should be positioned according to their size and rate of growth, using the more prolific ones to hide the filter and the back panel of the aquarium, and reserving the smaller varieties for the foreground : a 'centrepiece' such as an Amazon Sword can be included with pleasing effect.

Plants

To a considerable extent the choice of plants will be restricted to those available in your particular locality: unlike fish, they will not tolerate frequent changes of home without showing some reaction, such as shedding their leaves, or halting their growth for a time. Therefore your dealer is likely to stock plants in small numbers and keep only the more popular varieties so as to ensure a rapid turnover while they are still in good condition. While this will be more than adequate for the needs of most hobbyists, very lengthy lists are available from plant specialists who operate mail-order schemes: if you are seeking something out of the ordinary, or wish to purchase plants in considerable quantities, then look out for their advertisements in the aquatic magazines.

Like fish, plants have preferences for certain types of water, and the amount of light they need also varies. In practice the latter point is more important than the former, and almost any plant is worth trying if it appeals to the reader. Some plants are very hardy and rapid growers, and these are ideal, when the aquarium is first set up, to ensure a quick background of foliage. Others are much slower to establish themselves, or more delicate, and these can be experimented with at a later time when sheer volume of plants is not such an essential factor.

There are many thousands of species of plants suitable for aquatic growth, so naturally the following summary will have to be confined to the more popular ones.

Three groups are suggested, the divisions relating to the rôle of the plants in the aquarium:

Group A comprises those whose primary function is to provide a mass of foliage along the back and at the ends, effectively hiding the glass panels.

Group B consists of rather more interesting plants which can be placed individually or in small clusters around the aquarium, and whose growth is generally much less rapid than those in Group A.

Group C is reserved for those plants that are sufficiently imposing in appearance to merit the description of 'centrepiece', providing a magnificent focal point for the completed display.

On grounds of expense, quite apart from matters of practicality, it is unwise to attempt to stock the aquarium fully with plants when you initially set it up: far better to let them settle in and then spread naturally, for within a month or so they will have at least doubled in size.

For a 24 in. aquarium, it is suggested that the following are purchased:

Twenty plants or cuttings, selected from two or three of the varieties in Group A.

Ten plants or cuttings, selected from about five of the varieties in Group B.

One or two plants from Group C.

GROUP A
Vallisneria
This is one of the most popular grass-like aquatic plants, the leaves reaching from 10 in. to 15 in. in length. There are two main species: *Vallisneria spiralis* has straight leaves, while those of *Vallisneria torta* are spiral, like a corkscrew. An excellent background plant, but the lighting should not be too intense. Reproduces by means of runners on or just below the surface of the gravel.

Sagittaria
Another grass-like plant, but rather more hardy than Vallisneria — the leaves are too tough for most plant-eating fish to manage. *Sagittaria sinensis* (Giant Saggitaria) has broad, thick leaves, and is ideal for large aquaria: by contrast, *Sagittaria microfolia* reaches barely 2 in. or 3 in. in height, and soon forms an attractive carpet in the foreground. Also produces runners.

Ludwigia
A very fast-growing plant, with dark-green leaves on a central stem, it requires good lighting, and when it reaches the water surface it will still continue to

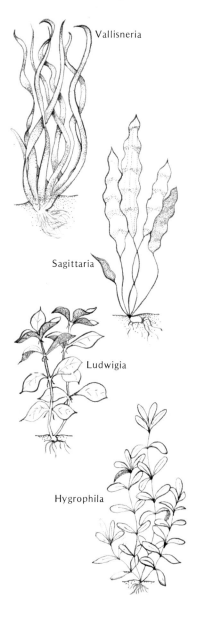

Vallisneria

Sagittaria

Ludwigia

Hygrophila

grow upwards since it is in reality a bog plant. Propagation is by means of cuttings, and it is advisable to discard the original stems periodically since they tend to become very woody and devoid of leaves on the lower part. A good beginner's plant, but it has a tendency to shed its leaves if something is amiss with its environment.

Hygrophila

Another fast-growing plant, the leaves being a little more pointed and a paler green than those of Ludwigia. Two popular species: *Hygrophila polysperma,* the more common, and *Hygrophila stricta,* the 'Giant' variety. Propagation is by means of cuttings, and if new growth is pruned and replanted regularly, pleasing 'bushes' of the plant may be maintained. *Hygrophila stricta* (Giant Hygrophila) remains upright on its strong central stem, and should be cut back occasionally otherwise it will grow out of the water. In some ways Hygrophila is superior to Ludwigia, as it is far less prone to unexpected leaf-shedding.

Elodea

Not a true tropical plant, being more often associated with coldwater aquaria, it will grow rapidly at 21-24 °C., but becomes very spindly and pale. It has little to recommend it other than its growth rate.

GROUP B
Limnophila (Ambulia)

A very attractive plant, with pale-green feathery leaves radiating out from a central stem; it requires moderate light, and, by taking cuttings and replanting them, can be kept bush-like. A fairly reliable grower.

Cabomba

Even more feathery and beautiful than Ambulia, and when in first-class condition is a brilliant green. Unfortunately it is a very temperamental

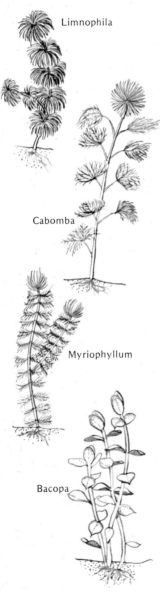

Limnophila

Cabomba

Myriophyllum

Bacopa

plant, needing strong light, ideally daylight. If it likes the conditions, it will grow quickly to the top of the aquarium and then wind around the surface, producing new shoots at intervals. These may be cut and planted when about 6 in. long.

Myriophyllum

Very fine leaves radiating out from a central stem, but uninspiring in colouration. Needing to be planted in bunches to create any effect, it then tends to accumulate mulm and other rubbish. An excellent plant for breeding fish, as it provides cover for either adhesive eggs or the fry of livebearers.

Bacopa

There are several species of this plant, but most are very similar in their general appearance: thick, rounded leaves situated in pairs at intervals along a rigid, brittle stem. Its bright colour and its curious appearance make Bacopa a worthy addition to any aquarium. Slow growing, propagated by cuttings.

Cryptocoryne

There many species of this plant, but probably no more than six or eight are widely available. They are relatively slow growing, and prefer to be left undisturbed: they will also do best under subdued lighting, such as in the shade of taller plants or where there are floating plants at the surface. Cryptocorynes are extremely popular, and no aquarium should be without two or three examples. The most common species are *Cryptocoryne beckettii* (one of the smallest), *C. griffithii, C. cordata, C. nevillii, C. harteliana* and *C. willisii.*

Ceratopteris (Indian Fern)

An unusual characteristic is the way the young of these plants are produced on the leaves of the parent: as the latter disintegrates, the young

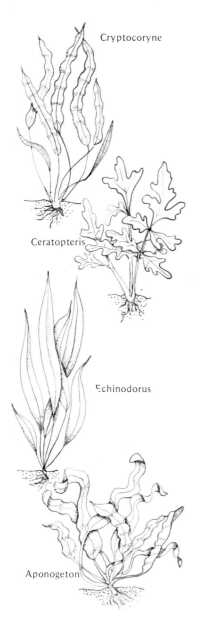

Cryptocoryne

Ceratopteris

Echinodorus

Aponogeton

float to the surface. When they have reached a reasonable size they may be planted in the gravel but if left floating, Ceratopteris makes one of the most interesting and least trouble-some of surface plants

Synnema triflorum (Water wisteria)

This is an attractive, fast growing and bushy plant — factors which ensure its popularity. Propagation is by cuttings, which quickly develop roots if left floating in the aquarium. Needs plenty of light.

GROUP C
Echinodorus

There are several large-growing species of Echinodorus, of which the most popular are *E. intermedius* — known as the Amazon Sword — and *E. radicans*. The Amazon Sword is probably the aquatic showpiece *par excellence,* reaching 18 in. or more in height, and comprising as many as two dozen leaves. *E. Radicans* is a steadier grower, producing heart-shaped leaves up to 3 in. or 4 in. across : each successive leaf will push a little nearer to the surface of the aquarium than its predecessors. Both of these species need strong light, but tend to develop algae growth on those portions nearest the light source.

Aponogeton

A. undulatum and *A. ulvaceus* are two of the most popular species, the edges of their leaves being attractively rippled. A third, more difficult species — *A. fenestralis* — is noteworthy for its lace-like latticework of veins which comprise the leaves, there being no normal tissue present. Aponogetons are rather brittle plants, easily dam-aged, and although they grow very luxuriantly for a time they may then halt their growth in anticipation of the dormant period, the time they rest in the wild when surrounding temper-atures fall.

Fish

The anatomy of fish

The hobbyist should be familiar with the main external features of his fish, if only to ensure that in conversation with other hobbyists he can understand the points being discussed. The fish illustrated is an imaginary one, portraying the features to be found on most species : however, variations from this are common — some do not have an adipose fin for example, while in others the ventral fins are modified to serve as 'feelers'.

Parts of a fish

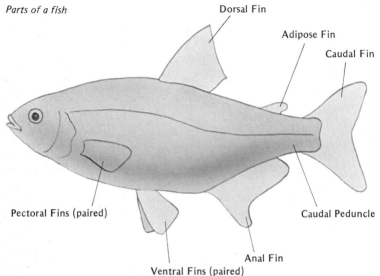

Dorsal Fin

Adipose Fin

Caudal Fin

Pectoral Fins (paired)

Caudal Peduncle

Anal Fin

Ventral Fins (paired)

'How many fish can I keep in my aquarium ?'

Overstocking the aquarium is one of the most common faults in fishkeeping, and one of which the author has often been guilty — albeit in misplaced enthusiasm for keeping a wider range of fish than space would really allow.

Many factors can influence the 'safe' number of fish that can be kept in a given size of aquarium, so a precise answer cannot be given. As a guide, and here we must err on the side of caution, you should allow one inch of fish (excluding the caudal fin, which is not normally counted when quoting a fish's size), to each twelve square inches of surface area. Thus an aquarium 24 in. x 12 in. x 15 in. high could accommodate 24 in. of fish — say 16 specimens with an average length of $1\frac{1}{2}$ in. If you buy your fish young, you must allow for the size they will eventually attain — which may be double the size at which you obtain them or larger. It is possible to crowd fish a little more than this as a short-term measure, particularly if aeration is used constantly, but their health must eventually suffer. They will become sickly and weak, one at a time, and subsequently die: in this way nature itself regulates the fish population to a level that can be readily supported in a given area. So ask yourself — do you want your fish uncrowded and healthy or crowded and unhealthy ? If the latter, they will surely be no credit to you as a fishkeeper.

Selecting the Fish

When the time arrives to purchase the first inhabitants for the aquarium, the enormity of choice in both species and varieties of fish can be quite overwhelming, and this complicates matters rather than simplifying them. Most of the species commonly available will live together quite happily, but there are certain exceptions that must be guarded against.

Much trouble can be avoided if the fish selected are all, when adult, of a roughly comparable size, for example between $\frac{3}{4}$ in. and $1\frac{1}{2}$ in., or between 1 in. and 2 in. This is obviously a generalisation: Corydoras catfish, for example, reaching approximately $2\frac{1}{2}$ in. length, are quite peaceful with any fish, with the exception perhaps of very young fry. By contrast, cichlids should generally never be put in with any fish smaller than themselves, and many of them are so vicious and spiteful, even with their own kind, that they have to be kept in 'solitary confinement'. Some species of catfish have such large mouths that they will swallow, whole, other fish only a little smaller than themselves. However, the interest that these particular fish create, both for the owner and for visiting fishkeepers, is often ample reward for the little extra attention they might require.

It is proposed to group the fishes into broad 'families', whose behaviour, characteristics, and requirements are likely to be very similar. The most common or interesting species will be referred to individually, identified by their Latin name — which every serious hobbyist should make a practice of using, since it avoids confusion and misunderstandings — and by the popular name where appropriate. This section cannot hope to cover all the fishes ever imported: rather, it is a guide to those species that deserve consideration for inclusion in the home aquarium. Which ones you actually select is a matter of purely personal taste, as it must always be, but it will naturally be governed by what is available for purchase in your locality at a particular time.

Livebearing Fish

This group could well be split into two sections: those that have been carefully bred and developed by man for many decades, so as to achieve particular colour combinations, fin shapes, and body contours — principally the Guppy, Platy, Swordtail, and Molly; and the remainder, those that have not been experimented with. Livebearers have always been popular in the community aquarium, perhaps because of the ease of raising their offspring. Unfortunately the quality of most of the 'man-made' species available has been steadily deteriorating, and the time may well have come when they can no longer be automatically recommended to the novice.

Swordtail *(Xiphophorus helleri)*. Found in a wide range of colours — Green, Gold, Albino, Red, Red Wagtail (red body with black finnage), and many more. Their common name originates from the sword-like extension that develops at the lower edge of the caudal fin in the male as it reaches maturity. The Swordtails commonly reach 3 in. in length, sometimes more, and as they have a tendency to bully smaller fish, care must be taken when including them in an aquarium.

Platy *(Xiphophorus maculatus)*. An attractive and lively little fish, usually reaching about $1\frac{1}{2}$ in. in length, found in many of the hues of the Swordtail — and a few more besides, perhaps the most attractive being the Yellow Wagtail variety. Peaceful and inquisitive by nature, platys are often regarded as the best choice amongst the livebearers for a community aquarium.

Black Molly *(Mollienesia sphenops)*. This is the only pure-black fish to be found in the home aquarium, and as such has a certain novelty value. Can grow quite large (3 in.), and enjoys browsing on soft algae often found on the plant leaves. Other species of Mollienesia include *M. velifera,* the males having a tall sail-like dorsal fin, and *M. latipinna.*

Guppy *(Poecilistes reticulatus)*. Renowned throughout the world for the brilliant colours and flowing finnage of the males. Can reach a length of $1\frac{1}{4}$ in. Females are quite drab, but much larger — up to 2 in. The most prolific of the livebearers, guppies are found in a wide variety of colour combinations: red, orange, or black being some of the dominant colours. Males will court and chase the females almost constantly, quite undeterred by the lack of response to their attentions. Not a particularly long-lived fish, and one that is usually purchased only at maturity, when the male's finnage is fully developed.

Mosquito Fish *(Heterandria formosa)*. An attractively marked fish, but lacking brilliant colouration. This is one of the smallest of the livebearers, the male reaching $\frac{3}{4}$ in., the female a little more: this, along with its peaceful disposition and rather shy nature, makes it an excellent choice for inclusion in a community aquarium of very small fish.

Blue Limia *(Limia melanogaster)*. Metallic-blue spangles on a dull olive background is this fish's obvious attraction, and when the male is mature this is supplemented by a series of dark bars on the rear part of the body, and a deep golden-yellow in the dorsal and caudal fins which are also edged with black. Maximum size of the female is around 2 in., the male rather less. A very lively species, and therefore one liking plenty of space. The triangular black marking on a young female's body should not be confused with the 'gravid spot' *(see the section on breeding livebearers)*.

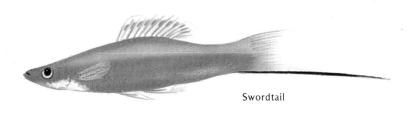

Swordtail

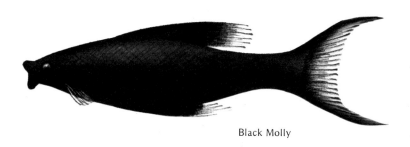

Black Molly

Guppy

Mosquito fish

Characins

The characin family includes some of the most suitable fishes for community aquaria: they are generally medium-sized, attractively coloured, peaceful and lively — though the feared and legendary Piranha is one obvious exception to this rule. Characins tend to have fairly small mouths in relation to the size of their bodies, and will accept almost any dried food together with the finer grades of live food. The smaller and more colourful species are perhaps seen at their best in shoals of a half dozen or more.

Neon Tetra *(Hyphessobrycon innesi)*. This fish is so well known that it is instantly recognised by everyone. A fairly streamlined fish, reaching little more than 1 in. in length, sporting a brilliant metallic-blue line running the length of the body, while a bright-red streak extends beneath the blue in the rear half of the body. Absolutely peaceful by nature, care has to be taken when introducing young specimens — often sold at barely $\frac{1}{2}$ in. length — into an established display, otherwise they will be regarded as a new 'live food' by the existing occupants. Neons are difficult to spawn, and it is even more of a challenge to hatch the eggs and raise the young: an almost complete absence of hardness of the water appears to be a prerequisite for breeding success with this species. Owing to the vast numbers that are bred abroad and imported, Neons are one of the least expensive of fish to buy.

Cardinal Tetra *(Cheirodon axelrodi)*. Almost identical to the Neon, this fish has the red streak extending the full length of the body, the result being an even more beautiful and striking appearance. Appreciably more expensive than its brother, and as a result not seen so frequently.

Glowlight Tetra *(Hyphessobrycon gracilis)*. As its popular name implies, the feature of this fish is a narrow golden-orange line running the entire length of the body: in young or out-of-condition specimens this may be rather pale, but in mature fish its brilliance is astonishing. A little larger than the neon, reaching $1\frac{1}{2}$ in., but still very peaceful, and a very worthwhile addition to a community aquarium.

Lemon Tetra *(Hyphessobrycon pulchripinnis)*. With a silver, laterally compressed body, this Tetra is not as dazzling as some of its relatives, but the contrast achieved by the splash of yellow on the anal fin and the semicircle of crimson around the eye make for an appealing and inexpensive community fish. It usually reaches $1\frac{1}{2}$ in. in length, and as in most characins, the easiest way to distinguish male from female is to look for the latter's much plumper body — virtually foolproof with mature specimens.

Serpae Tetra *(Hyphessobrycon callistus serpae)*. An attractive fish, the body a pale red or orange, with black markings on the dorsal fin, on the edge of the anal fin, and on the shoulder. Reputed by some occasionally to attack the fins of other fish, it should therefore not be put with others of lesser size than its own $1\frac{1}{2}$ in. Other less common but more peaceful relatives, with rather similar overall colouration, include *H. callistus minor*, *H. rubrostigma* (Bleeding Heart Tetra), and *H. rosaceus* (Rosy Tetra).

Flame Tetra *(Hyphessobrycon flammeus)*. The front half of the body is silver, the rear half a pale, but still distinct, red, the anal fin being edged with black. A very active fish, but sometimes inclined to chase others. Average size $1\frac{1}{4}$ in. $- 1\frac{1}{2}$ in.

Neon Tetra

Cardinal Tetra

Lemon Tetra

Flame Tetra

Pencil fish *(Nannostomus* and *Poecilobrycon* species).* The 'pencils' are very slender, peaceful, and rather shy fish, relying for appeal on their bold black markings with occasional touches of red, rather than on any particular brilliance. They will remain to all appearances quite motionless for lengthy periods, but on closer examination it will be seen that their almost transparent pectoral fins are beating away furiously, like the wings of an insect. The principal species are: *Nannostomus anomalus* $(1\frac{1}{2}$ in.), with a single black line running the length of the body; *N. marginatus* (1 in.), with two distinct black lines, and most of the fins touched with brilliant red patches; and *N. trifasciatus,* rather similar to the previous fish but reaching approximately $1\frac{1}{2}$ in. The *Poecilobrycons* are rather less common, the main species being *P. auratus, P. eques, P. harrisonii* and *P. unifasciatus:* all these would reach a length of 2 in. Some people keep a community aquarium devoted solely to pencil fish, perhaps including just a few other peaceful fish for colour, and there is no doubt that this is the answer if they are to look their best.

Penguin fish *(Thayeria sanctaemariae).* Bearing a thick black line the length of the body, and thence into the lower lobe of the caudal fin, the Penguin is an extremely lively and popular fish. However, it reaches 2 in. or more in length and, having a very healthy appetite — it will be one of the first to eat whatever food you put into the aquarium — it is advisable not to mix it with any very small fish: young neons, for example.

Black Widow *(Gymnocorymbus ternetzi).* An attractive fish, though its black colouration tends to fade with age. Like the Penguin, it should not be included with any very small fish. Average size, 2 in.

Silver Hatchet *(Gasteropelecus levis).* A plain silver body approximately 2 in. long, of unusual, almost semicircular shape, the eyes, mouth and pectoral fins being placed high up. Spends most of the time at or near the surface. Not the easiest fish to keep, and one that is unlikely to prove a worthwhile addition to a community aquarium. Very similar in shape is *Carnegiella strigata* (Marbled Hatchet), which is a little smaller at about $1\frac{1}{2}$ in.: the same cautions apply as for *G. levis.*

Blind Cave Fish *(Anoptichthys jordani).* This is an extremely interesting characin, originating from deep subterranean streams in Mexico: as no light ever penetrates into its native home the eyes became quite valueless and, over the course of countless generations, they disappeared. Instead, the Blind Cave Fish relies on its other highly developed senses, and can avoid rocks, find food and, apparently, spawn as successfully as any other fish. One further result of this lightless environment is that the body lacks any trace of pigment, showing up as a very pale pink. It grows rather large — $2\frac{1}{2}$ in. – 3 in. for a good example — but its peaceful nature makes it suitable for almost any aquarium. It is not a shy fish, and its healthy appetite is matched by few others.

Pencil fish

Penguin fish

Silver Hatchet

Blind Cave fish

47

Rasboras and Danios

These are the most active members of the aquarium, usually found racing energetically up and down within a few inches of the water surface. They are for the most part very easy to keep, peaceful in their behaviour, and quite beautiful when in fine condition: even the plain silvery areas of their bodies can shine like a mirror when they are at their best.

Harlequin *(Rasbora heteromorpha).* This must surely be the most popular rasbora, and quite understandably so. The body is deep, with a rich golden colour throughout: the hind part of the body carries a pure-black triangle, carefully following the outline of the fish so that there appears to be just a narrow edging of gold. The dorsal and anal fins show small streaks of red and black. Young fish are often quite unimpressive in colour, bearing little relationship to mature specimens: for best effect, as with so many of the smaller fishes, *R. heteromorpha* should be kept as a small shoal of at least six or eight fish. Not seen as often nowadays as the next fish.

Rasbora hengeli. This is what is often sold under the name Harlequin, yet in fact it is a fairly recent importation. It can be distinguished quite easily from the real Harlequin since it is not quite so deep bodied, the lower edge of the black triangle is distinctly concave, and the black and red streaks are absent from the fins. Having established that this fish is not really what it is usually advertised as, thereby inflicting on it a certain stigma, it is only fair to point out that it is, in the author's opinion at least, a far more beautiful fish than the original Harlequin. The golden gleam on the body is quite magnificent, particularly when seen in daylight, and, since it is one of the cheapest of the egglayers to purchase, it must surely deserve a place in every home. Like *R. heteromorpha,* it usually reaches a size of about $1\frac{1}{2}$ in.

Scissor-tail *(Rasbora trilineata).* A very active fish which reaches $2\frac{1}{2}$ in. – 3 in., and therefore should not be kept with any very small species. A plain silver body, the two lobes of the caudal fin each carrying a black patch edged with white: as the fish swims the fin alternately spreads and contracts, hence its popular name.

Rasbora borapetensis. A peaceful and elegant, rather than brilliant, fish reaching almost 2 in., the principal colouration being the black stripe running the length of the body, surmounted with another of silvery-gold.

Pygmy Rasbora *(Rasbora maculata).* Not the easiest of fish to keep, but one whose size (1 in. maximum) and attractive colours (pale red body with a few large black spots), make it a logical choice for inclusion in an aquarium holding smaller species.

Harlequin

Scissor tail

Zebra Danio *(Brachydanio rerio).* Its appearance is too well known to need further description, and not least of the factors accounting for its popularity is the ease with which it can be bred *(see section on breeding the egg-scatterers).* It is a fish that is perpetually on the move, usually with the male chasing the female. Maximum size $1\frac{3}{4}$ in.

Leopard Danio *(Brachydanio franki).* Very similar to the Zebra Danio, but the stripes of the former are here replaced with spots. Not quite so impressive or popular.

Pearl Danio *(Brachydanio albolineatus).* The whole of the body is suffused in tones reminiscent of mother-of-pearl, though when out of condition this may become just pinkish. Tends to look rather pale and insignificant in the aquarium. Size: $2\frac{1}{4}$ in.

Giant Danio *(Danio malabaricus).* As its name implies, the Giant Danio can reach over 4 in. in length. Its pattern forms a series of irregular pale-blue stripes set on a body colour of silver or cream. An excellent jumper.

White Cloud Mountain Minnow *(Tanichthys albonubes).* The whitish-blue stripe which runs the length of the body, so brilliant on young fish that many years ago they were called the 'Poor Man's Neon', tends to fade with maturity, leaving the red patches on the fins as the most prominent colour. Very easy to breed, and prefers temperatures around the 20-22°C. mark, although it will tolerate, with suitable acclimatisation, temperatures below 16°C.

Zebra Danio

Pearl Danio

Giant Danio

White-Cloud Mountain
Minnow

Barbs

This group of fish is generally very hardy and undemanding, and many of the species are relatively easy to breed — after a little experience with Zebras or White Clouds, perhaps. They do not like to be crowded, and since they are fast growing and hearty eaters, care should be taken in assessing the amount of space they need. There should be a place for barbs in almost every community aquarium, and when conditions are to their liking you will notice an enormous improvement in their colouration.

Tiger Barb *(Barbus tetrazona)*. Perhaps the most popular of all barbs — certainly the most dashing, with its broad black bars and bright red fins. The female, in common with most barbs, is appreciably plumper in the body at maturity, whilst the male will have the more intense red colouration. An occasional specimen may be found to be a little spiteful, so caution would dictate that they should not be included with other fish much less than their own 2 in. length.

Checker Barb *(Barbus oligolepsis)*. An attractive, though not brilliant, fish, its popular name being due to the pattern of black markings on its flanks. Males carry a black edging to the dorsal and caudal fins, a feature absent on the females. Very peaceful, reaching $1\frac{1}{2}$ in. in length.

Cherry Barb *(Barbus titteya)*. The intense dark cherry-red colour adopted by the male at breeding time is very beautiful, and quite different from his normal markings. At 2 in., a small and rather shy fish, but one of the best of the barbs for the community aquarium.

Tiger Barb

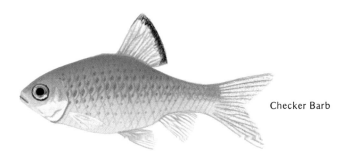

Checker Barb

Cherry Barb

53

Golden Barb *(Barbus schuberti)*. The whole body is a matt golden-yellow, the fins being various shades of red : the belly has more of a metallic, silver hue. The male carries a row of dark blotches running backwards from the shoulder along the upper flanks, while the female merely has a few indistinct dark spots on the upper half of the body. This fish is long lived, usually reaches little more than 2 in., and provides a beautiful contrast with the dark greens of the aquarium plants.

Half-banded Barb *(Barbus semifasciolatus)*. As the newer, more colourful fish are imported, so the older favourites lose their popularity : this is one fish that has so suffered. The body is a pale gold, and has a number of incomplete narrow black bars. An ideal community fish, and one that is easy to breed ; its size is a little greater than *B. schuberti.*

Rosy Barb *(Barbus conchonius)*. The easiest of barbs to spawn, yet today it is becoming almost a rarity — again, because tastes have changed. In young specimens the body is a plain silver, with a black spot just forward of the caudal peduncle. As they mature, the females take on an olive colouration, darkest on the upper surfaces : the males develop a burnished-copper hue over the entire body, save for the green on the upper parts, and black patches on the dorsal, anal, and ventral fins. The Rosy Barb is perhaps a little large for many aquaria : a good specimen can reach a full 3 in.

Ruby Barb/Nigger Barb *(Barbus nigrofasciatus)*. Like the Cherry Barb, the male Ruby Barb undergoes a transformation of colour at breeding time, the pale golden body turning a brilliant deep red, the black markings becoming even more profound. Young specimens may be confused at fist glance for Tiger Barbs, though the black bars are far less clean-cut, and there is no red edging to the dorsal. A peaceful, medium-size fish, reaching $2\frac{1}{2}$ in., but one that is not often seen nowadays.

Half-banded Barb

Rosy Barb

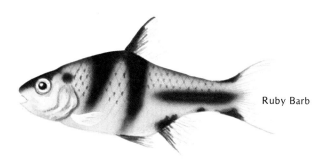

Ruby Barb

55

Cichlids

Cichlids are often regarded as being the most intelligent of the smaller freshwater fish, having more highly developed senses than the others. Although this may be true, they are not good community fish. Among the most important reasons for this we can include the following:

They grow to a very considerable size: many will reach 6 in. or more, and even those known as 'Dwarf' Cichlids will usually be at least $2\frac{1}{2}$ in. in length. They are strongly territorial by nature — often aggressively so, fighting off intruders who invade their part of the aquarium. They also tend to dig up the gravel, piling it into heaps, uprooting the plants, and generally creating chaos.

Many species turn out to be vicious bullies, even with their own kind. And they will rarely eat dried or flaked food, preferring live foods, small morsels of meat, and, naturally, any small fish that happen to stray close enough.

Having stressed these points, it must be said that they make quite fascinating inmates for any subsequent aquarium that the hobbyist might set up, providing they have the extra space and attention that they need. Many of the cichlids are quite easy to breed — some are far too prolific — since they generally care for their eggs and young with a devotion exceeding that found even in the human race.

Blue Acara *(Aequidens latifrons).* The predominant colour of this fish is a metallic green, appearing as 'spangles' over most of the flanks and upper part of the body: there are additionally some rather darkish patches on the body, the intensity of these being very variable. In common with most cichlids, it is fairly easy to distinguish the sex in mature specimens, the male having rather longer points on the dorsal and anal fins. The easiest cichlid to breed, and tolerably peaceful with others of a similar size, it can reach up to 6 in., though is more usually seen at around 4 in.

Marbled Cichlid *(Astronotus ocellatus).* When small this is a very beautiful fish, with its variable black — and cream — marbled body colours: in large specimens — it can reach a foot long — the sharpness of its markings is lost. Rather aggressive, and a little temperamental over changes in water conditions.

Festive Cichlid *(Cichlasoma festivum).* One of the most peaceful of the larger cichlids, it has a plain silver or pale olive-green body dominated by an angular black stripe running from the tip of the dorsal fin, through the eye, to the mouth. Can be kept with the larger barbs, usually reaching 4 in. – 5 in.

Cichlasoma severum. Similar in its peaceful nature to the Festive Cichlid and a little larger, the colour is very variable in both intensity and shade: usually the body will be a pale brown, with six or seven faint bars appearing. In maturity, the males develop rows of reddish-brown spots on the flanks and head.

Jewel Cichlid *(Hemichromis bimaculatus).* Despite its exceptionally vicious nature, the incredible beauty of the Jewel Cichlid has endeared it to many hobbyists. The brilliant red body of the male in breeding condition, overlaid with spangles of metallic blue, is a sight that is never forgotten: at times the colour of the female is almost a match for her mate. They are ready breeders, and should be kept on their own with ample rocks and flower pots for refuge. Maximum size 4 in., but will breed at much less than this.

Blue Acara

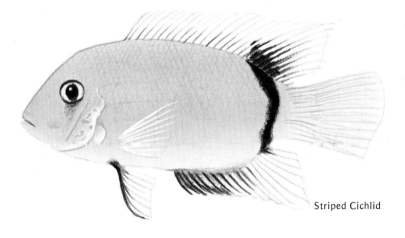

Striped Cichlid

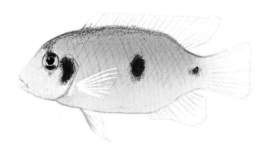

Jewel Cichlid

57

Angel Fish *(Pterophyllum* species). This is, along with the Neon Tetra and the Siamese Fighter, perhaps the best known of all tropical fish. Its long, flowing fins and graceful movement epitomise the most tranquil aspects of the hobby. Yet, being a cichlid, the Angel Fish is not as perfect a companion as its name might imply. Although most Angels are purchased with a body size of little more than $\frac{3}{4}$ in. across, they can all too quickly grow to the diameter of a champagne glass, with an 8 in. spread of fins. This means that care must be taken to provide an aquarium large enough for their needs, and also to make sure that they will not be permanently kept with any very small fish, say under $1\frac{1}{2}$ in., that they might soon come to regard as a meal. Fortunately they are not vicious, but their flowing fins offer a tempting target for fin-nippers such as some of the other cichlids and tiger barbs. As adult fish, they are best kept with their own kind, just three or four in a well-planted 24 in. long aquarium. There are several colour varieties including silver, black, and golden : some types also have considerably extended finnage.

Dwarf Cichlids. A number of genera of fish, principally *Apistogramma, Nannacara* and *Pelmatochromis,* are commonly referred to as 'Dwarf Cichlids'. These fish are, as implied, usually smaller than other cichlids, though some *Pelmatochromis* species are 5 in. – 6 in. long; they are more territorially inclined, and within their territories, are of a more peaceful disposition. This means that in an aquarium of reasonable size — 36 in. or 48 in. long — and well stocked with rocks and flower pots laid on their side, one can have pairs of perhaps four or five species living in harmony : they may even spawn and raise a brood of young in their own particular enclave. This can be a very interesting project, and the most suitable fish would include *Apistogramma agassizi, A. ornatipinnis, Nannacara anomala* and *Pelmatochromis kribensis. Apistogramma ramirezi* is another beautiful fish, but will not thrive if water conditions fail to meet its requirements. With Apistogramma and Nannacara species, it should be possible to plant the aquarium normally : those of the genus Pelmatochromis are rather more likely to move the gravel around as they 'rearrange' their home.

Angel fish

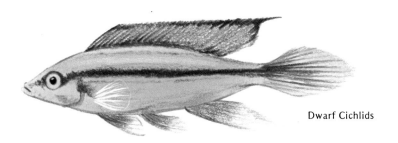

Dwarf Cichlids

Labyrinths

Labyrinths are a group of fish which possess an auxiliary air-breathing organ to supplement the oxygen they extract from the water in the normal way, and may be observed approaching the water surface periodically to take a gulp of air. They are generally very partial to live foods, in preference to dried types, and a tendency, shared by many of the species, to bully and harrass the other occupants will be minimised if their stomachs are kept well filled. This group of fish has a particular susceptibility to dropsy if kept in overcrowded or unsatisfactory conditions, and also, in similar circumstances, to boils on the head or body.

Siamese Fighter *(Betta splendens)*. A very well-known and very beautiful fish, the male has long, flowing fins coloured in brilliant red, blue, or green — or various combinations. The female has much shorter finnage and her colours are rather more drab. The males, as the popular name suggests, will attack each other on sight; a pugnacious attitude which is often extended to other fish as well; but since their flowing fins are an ideal target for bullies they are rarely at their best in a community aquarium — they will usually be found hiding behind some rocks or clump of plants, looking a very sad sight indeed. If a small aquarium can be devoted solely to a pair of Siamese Fighters, then they are seen at their best: they are also one of the simplest and most interesting fish to breed. Body length approximately $2\frac{1}{2}$ in.

Dwarf Gourami *(Colisa lalia)*. The male is generally acknowledged as the most beautiful of the gouramis, with his narrow bars of red and blue shining in the sunlight: his mate is far more drab, but bears traces of similar markings. It is a rather delicate fish, and really good specimens are difficult to come across: it is a ready spawner, but the young fry are particularly difficult to raise beyond about the seventh day. Reaches 2 in. in length.

Thick-lip Gourami *(Colisa labiosa)*. This fish is a little larger than the Dwarf Gourami, and generally far hardier. The male has pale-red and green bars on the body, rather similar to the Dwarf, but in maturity the body becomes much darker and the dorsal and anal fins are edged with yellow. The female has much of the colour of an immature male, together with a rounded tip to her dorsal fin — that of the male is pointed. Perhaps the best Gourami for a community aquarium.

Leeri, Pearl, Lace or Mosaic Gourami *(Trichogaster leeri)*. At 4 in. – 5 in., a medium-sized fish, but quite peaceful. The whole body is covered with a fine lace-like patterning, and a dark line from the eye peters out just before it reaches the caudal peduncle. The mature male develops a vivid orange colour around the head and throat. A beautiful fish, but inclined to be shy; and sometimes susceptible to changes in water conditions.

Three-Spot Gourami *(Trichogaster trichopterus)*. This fish derives its popular name from the two dark blobs on the body, one near the caudal peduncle and the other on its middle flanks, with its dark eye making the third spot. Commonly seen on sale at about $1\frac{1}{2}$ in. in length, when they are sufficiently attractive for considerable numbers to be purchased. But they can reach 6 in. or more in length in a short time and, unless their companions are of a similar size, the tranquility of the display will be destroyed. Not recommended for the novice, though they are very suitable for inclusion in large display aquaria.

Paradise Fish *(Macropodus opercularis)*. A very hardy and popular fish from the early days of tropical fishkeeping, but too aggressive and large to mix in with today's favourites. Colouration is rather similar to the young *Colisa labiosa* but the body is far less deep.

Siamese Fighter

Dwarf Gourami

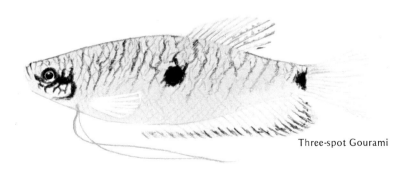

Three-spot Gourami

Catfish

This group of fish, so called because of the 'whiskers' that most of them sport around the mouth, is extremely diverse in size, temperament, and behaviour. Some — the *Corydoras,* for example — are exceedingly peaceful, hardy, attractively marked, and sociable little creatures: others are much less suitable for the community aquarium, being secretive, large, and with mouths that can — and will — swallow any of the more dainty inhabitants swimming close by. With catfish perhaps more than with any other fish, beware of purchasing a specimen that you cannot identify as being of a peaceful disposition: a good example of what happens if this warning is ignored can be found with the many thousands of the genus *Clarias* that were imported a few years ago. Usually purchased from the dealer at about $1\frac{1}{2}$ in. in length, they would grow and grow, and gradually all the other fish in the aquarium would disappear: eventually all that remained was a solitary, beautiful *Clarias* catfish, between 10 in. and 18 in. long, that could not be kept with anything else. When American owners started releasing these unwanted specimens in the wild, the native fish themselves were in danger of extinction, so much so that strict controls had to be introduced.

Corydoras species. There are more than a dozen common species of Corydoras catfish, and most will reach approximately $2\frac{1}{2}$ in. in length. They are energetic feeders, foraging for particles of food amongst the gravel with their slightly protruding mouths: this will rarely disturb the plants, but the gravel itself tends to become levelled in time. They will happily accept dried food, though tubifex worms are their particular favourite. The most popular species are *C. aeneus,* a pinkish body underneath, with metallic green around the head and flanks; *C. paleatus,* a pale body colour overlaid with irregular patches of dark olive-green; *C. julii,* known as the Leopard Corydoras, with rows of small black spots on a cream-coloured body; and *C. arcuatus,* whose pale body has a curved black line running over the shoulder from the eye to the caudal peduncle. There are many other species featuring dark-spotted patterns of various descriptions, and these markings give the catfish an appearance that may best be described as cute; and all are equally suitable for the aquarium. The one oddity is **Dwarf Corydoras** *(C. hastatus),* reaching around $1\frac{1}{2}$ in. and tending to swim more in midwater — something the other species rarely do.

Talking Catfish *(Acanthadoras spinosissimus).* This fish derives its name from the grunting noises it makes when lifted out of the water: care must be taken when catching it with a net to prevent the numerous spines on its body from getting caught in the mesh. It is an ugly fish to some tastes, spending most of its time hidden away under a rock in some corner. Live food is essential, preferably tubifex, at least two or three times a week. Average size 3 in. – 4 in.

Hoplosternum thoracatum. One of the larger catfish suitable for the community aquarium, commonly reaching 6 in. in length. Its body is attractively mottled with dark brown on a light fawn background: the mouth is small and adapted for foraging deep into the gravel. Along with *H. littorale* — whose body colour is a drab dark grey — it appreciates plenty of space to swim in. Can be kept with fish of $1\frac{1}{2}$ in. or larger with safety: males can be recognised by the upward-turning of the ends of the thick first ray of the pectoral fins.

Sucker-mouthed Catfish. There are a number of catfish that possess a rounded mouth placed on the underside of the head, similar to a sucker in appearance: with this mouth they can attach themselves to plant leaves, rocks, or the glass sides of the aquarium, while at the same time using the rasp-like

Bronze Catfish

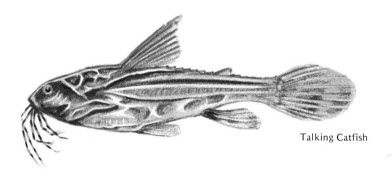

Talking Catfish

63

inner parts of the mouth to remove algae growing on the surface. They are primarily vegetarian in their diet, which means they will keep the aquarium virtually clear of any unwanted and unsightly algae, providing, of course, that it is not growing too excessively. Some of these catfish, principally *Otocinclus affinis* and *O. vittatus,* remain small and peaceful, rarely exceeding $1\frac{1}{2}$ in.

Others, such as those of the genera *Plecostomus, Xenocara, Ancistrus,* and *Loricaria,* can reach 8 in. or more, and while they may occasionally spar with each other they will rarely prove troublesome to unrelated occupants of the aquarium, whatever their size. They will generally make their appearance when things are quiet and still, usually after dark, and so their full beauty is rarely appreciated. Members of the genus *Plecostomus,* in particular, have the most elegant, sail-like dorsal fins, together with caudal fins of almost equal proportions when fully extended. Colours range from a light-brown speckled body, through the dark browns to a dark slate-grey. Precise identification is often difficult with this group of fish, but since they are all of a very similar disposition this should not create undue problems. The function they fulfil in the aquarium, in keeping unsightly algae to a minimum, is sufficiently important to outweigh their considerable cost: if you have room, keep one in each aquarium — you will not be disappointed.

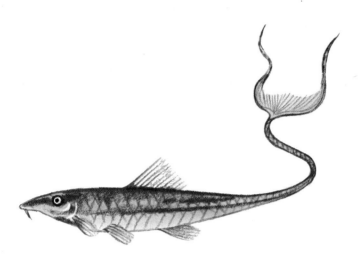

Whiptail Catfish

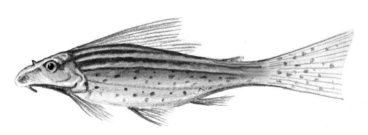

Plecostomus commersoni

Killifish (Tooth Carps)

The principal genera of this group are *Aphyosemion, Aplocheilus, Epiplatys,* and *Rivulus,* and include, according to many people, some of the most beautiful of all freshwater tropical fish. As a general rule the males are much brighter, have longer fins, and are a little more belligerent by nature than the females: in fact, in some species the latter are quite drab, mundane, and shy by comparison. Despite their obvious points of appeal, Killifish cannot be regarded as suitable for inclusion in a normal community aquarium since they exist almost entirely on live foods, which may not always be conveniently available. The most important factor weighing against their greater popularity is the particular water conditions — very soft and rather acid — that they prefer: for many of them, in fact, such water is absolutely essential if they are to survive for any length of time. Providing conditions are to their liking and they are kept, ideally, only with their own kind, many of the Killifish are not difficult to breed: with some species the eggs have to be dried out in a special way for many months before water is added and the young fry emerge — a unique method of creating the following generation, but one which duplicates the particular circumstances found in the wild.

To repeat the point, Killifish are not really community fish, nor are they particularly suitable for beginners: in time, if the beautiful colours of these fish take your fancy, there are specialist Killifish groups in many parts of the country which can assist you.

Miscellaneous Others

The author makes no apologies for now including a section of rather less common fish, which are for the most part his own particular favourites. The fact that they are not so often seen does not make them any less suitable contenders for a place in the home aquarium — in fact they often add much to the display by virtue of their individuality.

Bumble Bee Goby *(Brachygobius xanthozona).* An attractive fish, rarely exceeding $1\frac{1}{2}$ in., that very closely resembles a bee with its broad bands of yellow and black. A somewhat inactive creature, spending most of the time on the bottom, it needs a regular diet of live food: if this is not forthcoming it has a tendency to attack the fins of other fish, but more often it will waste away and die.

Botia sidthimunki. The smallest of the botias, and one that does not have the secretive and bullying nature common to the larger of the species. Its black and silver markings are not brilliant, yet it has a particular appeal when kept with other fish of a similarly peaceful disposition. Accepts dried food, but appreciates an occasional treat of live daphnia or tubifex: usually grows to approximately $1\frac{1}{2}$ in.

Striped Botia *(Botia strigata).* Attractively marked with narrow bands of pale yellow and dark brown, this fish usually attains a length of around $2\frac{1}{2}$ in. Its behaviour is peaceful and lively, though a little shy when newly introduced to an aquarium. An excellent community fish.

Kuhli Eel *(Acanthophthalmus semicinctus).* There are several species referred to as the Kuhli Eel, and this is the most common: a long snake-like body having alternate bands of pale yellow and black on the top and flanks, and with a pink underbelly. A very active fish, reaching $3\frac{1}{2}$ in., it is perhaps one of the most difficult to catch in a planted aquarium.

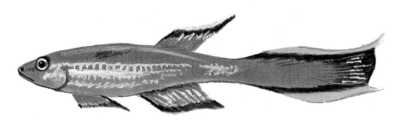

Lyretail

Rivulus cylindraceus

Bumble Bee Goby

Spiny Eels *(Mastacembelus* species). This group of eel-like fishes, all featuring pointed heads, tapering bodies, and apparently very small mouths, includes species that can exceed 24 in. in length, though those usually seen in aquaria are in the range 5 in. – 9 in. Although the mouth appears quite small, and carries a proboscis-like extension, it can suck in small worms and even any unwary small fish that might come too close : a shoal of Neon Tetras possessed by the author disappeared in this way before the culprit was actually caught in the act. As a result, this particular Spiny Eel is now kept well-fed, and far away from small fish. Live food is absolutely essential, small worms being eagerly accepted by the larger specimens. Spiny Eels have a tendency to burrow into the gravel when frightened, but rarely uproot any plants in the process.

Sucking Loach *(Gyrinocheilus aymonieri).* One of the best fish for clearing excess algae from plant leaves and rocks, and quite inexpensive too. Tolerant of a wide range of water conditions, it can reach well over 6 in. in length, though fortunately it is usually found rather smaller than this. Although rather secretive when people are near, when quiet returns it will dart rapidly around looking for food. Ideal for the community aquarium, but an occasional specimen, particularly if poorly fed, will attach itself with its sucker-like mouth onto the side of a large, slow-swimming fish such as an Angel : if this is done repeatedly, the victim may suffer serious damage.

Red-tailed Black Shark *(Labeo bicolor).* Its popular name is an accurate enough description, though it is of course nothing like the true shark. It has a streamlined, though solid, body, and commonly reaches 4 in. in length : all its fins, except the pectorals, are pigmented — the caudal a bright red, the others matching the body colour of dark grey or black. Usually feeds on algae, but equally fond of dried or live foods. *L. bicolor* is becoming very expensive, and as an alternative the Red-finned Shark, *L. erythrura,* is enjoying some popularity.

LIFE-SPAN OF FISH

It is doubtful whether one fish in a hundred ever attains what might be regarded as a ripe old age — the vast majority die prematurely from overcrowding when imported, disease, neglect, bullying or occasionally from some accidental cause. Perhaps because of this fact, many people seem to think that it is exceptional for a tropical fish, given the right conditions, to live the number of years achieved by other household pets.

Within families of fish we can accept a general rule that the life-span is broadly related to the fish's adult size, a larger size tending to indicate a longer life. However there is considerable variation by family. The livebearers, characins, danios, and rasboras will have a life span broadly in the range of two to six years. Barbs, botias, and labyrinths fare rather better with a range of three to eight years, and cichlids may even extend a little further than this. But it is the catfish that really take the prize for longevity : even the small corydoras can reach six or eight years, and the larger species can comfortably run to double figures.

Kuhli Eel

Sucking Loach

Feeding

'A pinch a day' — so runs the old maxim on the feeding of fish. And we all know just how vague and misleading a piece of advice like that can turn out to be. Fish are like humans: at one extreme they can have such little, or unsuitable, food that malnutrition results, at the other they can have so much that they cannot manage to eat it all, and it goes bad. Between these extremes there is a very wide range of 'correct' feeding, and provided that this latitude is respected there should be no problems. Fish, being relatively small creatures, need feeding regularly: once a day is ideal, but if they are young this can be stepped up to two, three, or even more, feedings to achieve maximum growth rate. But, however many times you feed them, ensure that all the food is eaten and not merely lying amongst the gravel within two or three minutes: and this naturally means that if you are feeding several times each day, the quantity given for each occasion must be correspondingly less. Any uneaten food, with the possible exception of some live foods given in slight excess, must start to pollute within a few hours at tropical aquarium temperatures: and this, if done with any regularity, will turn the gravel into a stinking, black mass, killing the fish as a result.

Types of Food

Fish will eat almost anything normally eaten by humans — meat, fish, vegetables, cereal, and even egg — provided it is sufficiently fine for them to swallow without choking, and it does not dissolve or break-up too readily. However, from the point both of convenience and nutritional value it would be hard to improve on the proprietary dried foods, often in a flake form, which are so readily available: they are also very economical, particularly for just one or two aquaria. If you do get to the stage of having large numbers of fish, or keeping those with hefty appetites, such as cichlids and barbs, then it may be worthwhile to prepare your own food. Home-drying of meat and other foods destroys much of the nourishment and almost all of the appeal from the viewpoint of the fish: but those with a freezing compartment in their refrigerator can keep a supply of home-made food always to hand. From my own experience the following is a very economical formula, and the fish take it with great delight.

Open a tin of good-quality, all-meat dog food: remove any excess fat, gristle, and gravy, and then use a hand-operated

Daphnia

Daphnia

Small aquatic crustaceans, commonly known as the 'water fleas', and found in the wild in ponds. May be collected with a fine net, but beware of unwanted pests such as leeches and insect larvae that may be caught at the same time.

Mosquito Larvae

Found in water butts and other static bodies of water during the summer, they are easily caught with a fine net and provide excellent food for medium-sized fish.

Tubifex

An aquatic worm, perhaps 1 in. in length, that lives in the mud near the sewage outfalls of large rivers. Since it is often found in water too polluted for higher forms of aquatic life to survive, it has acquired the undeserved reputation of introducing disease into the aquarium. Should be kept in a bucket or bowl under a slowly running tap to keep it fresh: each day drain most of the water out of the container, then refill with a jet of water, breaking up the ball-like cluster of tubifex worms in the process. When they have settled on the bottom, drain off the water again and repeat the process. When they have again settled, take out whatever you require for feeding, and refill the container with water: in this way you can be sure of getting live tubifex worms, quite free of contamination. Although they will live for a long time in the aquarium, burrowed deep into the gravel, you should feed them in only small quantities at a time.

Catfish in particular love these worms, but they will prove a little large for the very small fish: in this case, they may be roughly chopped up with a razor blade before being put into the aquarium.

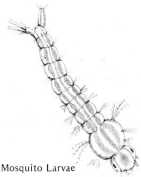

Mosquito Larvae

Tubifex worms

vegetable chopper to reduce it almost to a purée. Mix in well a small spoonful of baby cereal, put into containers and freeze : small pieces can be put into the aquarium, still frozen, and the fish will bite pieces off as they thaw out. It is an excellent food — either regularly provided or as an occasional treat. Other foods that can be given occasionally include a tinned pea, squashed between finger and thumb; a little finely chopped cooked liver; frozen prawn, similarly chopped; and tinned cod roe. But always remember that the fish will need only minute quantities, and remove any that is left uneaten after five minutes. Like humans, your fish will appreciate a little variety in their eating habits.

Live foods are regarded by some people as indispensible for the well-being of the fish, and by others as too much of a bother to worry about. Whilst the former is not strictly true, there is no doubt about the obvious enjoyment the fish get from such a treat, and the latter viewpoint is perhaps equally misleading.

White worms
About $\frac{1}{2}$ in. long, these are cultivated at home in a shallow box of earth : a small square of moistened bread is laid on the surface of the earth, and the worms cluster underneath to consume it. The box should be covered with a sheet of glass and kept in a cool, dark place, though not too cold. You must purchase an initial 'culture' of the worms to get started.

Grindal Worms
Rather smaller than white worms, they prefer conditions that are a little warmer and damper. In their case a small quantity of baby cereal is sprinkled over the surface of the earth, and the worms may be carefully scraped up when they have consumed it.

Micro Worms
Minute aquatic worms, ideal for feeding very young fish. Prepare a small quantity of cooked porridge or baby cereal, and put it in a $\frac{1}{2}$ in. layer in a plastic sandwich box : when cool add a couple of drops from an existing micro culture and replace the lid. About five days later the surface will be teeming with these minute creatures, which will start to crawl up the side of the box: they can be transferred to the aquarium with a clean finger or a small brush, the equivalent of a drop or two containing many thousands of the worms. The culture will only last about ten days before it goes bad, so it is best to have two or three boxes started at intervals. Should be kept at a warm room temperature.

Breeding

It will not be too long before the novice succumbs to the almost irresistible urge to breed some of the fish he owns, and often this is sparked off by the sight of one or two miniscule youngsters that have found the safety of a clump of floating plants to escape the hungry mouths of the other fish in the aquarium.

For many of the popular species the challenge comes more from raising the fry — the term used for very young fish — than from actually producing them in the first place. We can group the fish into two broad categories according to their method of reproduction: the viviparous, or livebearers, where the eggs, after fertilization, develop within the female and fully formed miniature fish are born. Then there are the ovoparous, the egg layers, which produce eggs that are fertilized and develop away from the female. There are many variations of detail within these broad categories, and for that reason it is proposed to mention selected species that are representative, in their breeding patterns, of genera or whole families of fish.

Livebearers
The first problem, naturally enough, is to distinguish the male from the female, and this is usually a very simple job (*see diagrams on p. 74*).

Most of the livebearers will produce young fish at fairly regular intervals — around twenty-eight days, depending on the temperature — ranging in numbers from about twenty-five for a young female to a hundred or two for a large adult. Guppys and Platies fit into this pattern, and so do Mollies and Swordtails with one exception: if conditions are not quite to their liking they can delay the birth, either for a few days or on occasions almost indefinitely. A few less-popular species of livebearers will produce their young over a much longer period, dropping two or three each day over a period of ten days or so: the Mosquito fish and Half-beaks may be included here.

One surprising point is that the female livebearer can produce as many as six or eight broods from just a single mating, apparently storing the spermatazoa from the male for lengthy periods.

Having established that the livebearers produce their young with reasonable regularity, the problem is one of ensuring that they are not promptly eaten, either by the mother or by any other fish

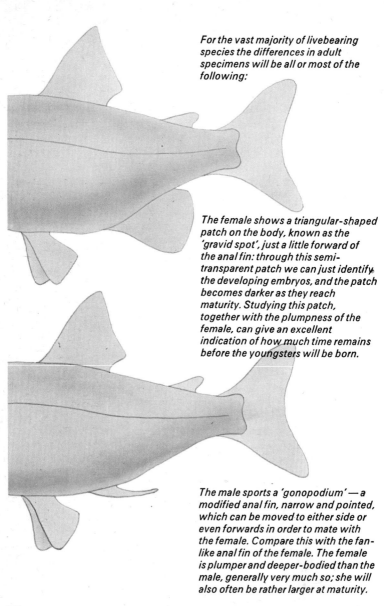

For the vast majority of livebearing species the differences in adult specimens will be all or most of the following:

The female shows a triangular-shaped patch on the body, known as the 'gravid spot', just a little forward of the anal fin: through this semi-transparent patch we can just identify the developing embryos, and the patch becomes darker as they reach maturity. Studying this patch, together with the plumpness of the female, can give an excellent indication of how much time remains before the youngsters will be born.

The male sports a 'gonopodium' — a modified anal fin, narrow and pointed, which can be moved to either side or even forwards in order to mate with the female. Compare this with the fan-like anal fin of the female. The female is plumper and deeper-bodied than the male, generally very much so; she will also often be rather larger at maturity.

present. On birth the fry will fall quickly to the bottom of the aquarium where they will remain for a while, hardly moving and quite defenceless. After perhaps an hour or so they will have gathered sufficient strength to find hiding places, and providing the aquarium is fairly heavily planted they have some chance of survival against all but the most persistent of enemies.

It is obviously best to keep an aquarium specially for the purpose of breeding livebearers, but it is equally obvious that if all the young survive they will need a lot of space for growing, over a period of three or four months, and the owner will then need to find a suitable outlet for them. Good, well-grown specimens of many of the popular livebearers, Guppys excluded, will often be welcomed by a local dealer: although he will not be prepared to pay much for them, it does provide the opportunity to get back a small contribution towards the cost of their feeding. If the hobbyist does not want to get inundated with young fish, and the need to buy further tanks, one idea is to move all the youngsters out of the breeding tank into the main aquarium at about one week of age: many will get eaten, but the fittest will survive to replace those that die of old age. This may appal some people, but it is, after all, the system that operates in the wild.

One word of caution: there are available some small transparent plastic boxes — known as breeding traps — into which the female is placed to produce her young. These are cruel devices, often frightening the fish so much that either the young are born dead, or she herself dies. Furthermore, if any attempt is made to raise the fry in the box they will be stunted — there is insufficient room and an inadequate circulation of fresh water for there to be any other result. If such a device is needed in the aquarium, ensure it is of the plain net-covered type which, if a few sprigs of plant are included, affords some chance of success in breeding small quantities of livebearers without the need for a separate aquarium.

Egglayers
These involve far more work and expertise than livebearers, and a separate breeding tank is absolutely essential. Not only do we have to ensure that the conditions are suitable for the parents themselves, so as to encourage the spawning, but subsequently we have to cope with perhaps as many as a thousand minute, splinter-like creatures whose demands are far more critical. While the livebearing young are shielded and sheltered within the female until they have achieved almost complete self-sufficiency, the fry of the

Breeding tank

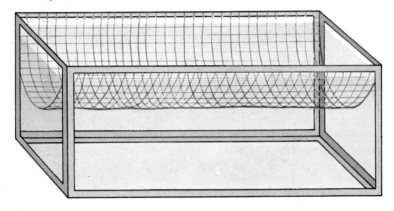

This tank should be of adequate dimensions — an 18 in. x 12 in. x 12 in. or 24 in. x 12 in. x 12 in. will suffice for most species — and be kept at 25-27 °C., just a few degrees above the temperature to which the fish have been accustomed.

Water mix

The water can be one third from the existing aquarium, two thirds fresh from the tap: this combination of slightly increased temperature and fresh water will often encourage spawning, as will an hour or so of early morning sunshine falling on the breeding tank. The addition of a jar or two of peat water — water in which pure peat has been allowed to stand for a couple of days and then filtered off — will acidify conditions slightly, and this may also be an encouragement if success remains elusive.

egglayers emerge into a world which is totally inhospitable — hence the need to produce a large number of eggs at a time to ensure survival of the species.

Accurate sexing of the adult fish is naturally vital, and since the male egglayers lack the anal fin modification of their livebearer counterparts, it is a task which for many species can only be done when the fish are mature and in first-class health — in other words, in breeding condition. The differences between male and female can be quite subtle and may vary from genus to genus: the female almost always being rather plumper, while the male may be more intense in his colouration, or his dorsal and ventral fins a little more pointed. Another indication is the male chasing after the female, which often occurs in a well-kept community aquarium: the aim will then be to disturb them as little as possible when transferring them to the breeding tank. This tank should be of adequate dimensions — an 18 in. x 12 in. x 12 in. or 24 in. x 12 in. x 12 in. will suffice for most species — and kept at 25-27 °C., just a few degrees above the temperature to which the fish have been accustomed. The water can be one third from the existing aquarium, two thirds fresh from the tap: this combination of slightly increased temperature and fresh water will often encourage spawning, as will an hour or so of early morning sunshine falling on the breeding tank. The addition of a jar or two of peat water — water in which pure peat has been allowed to stand for a couple of days and then filtered off — will acidify conditions slightly and this may also be an encouragement if success remains elusive.

It should be remembered that one cannot give a hard-and-fast rule to cover the needs of all fish, and individual species may have requirements marginally or substantially different.

Although there is a degree of uniformity in the way that we raise these fry, the actual spawning processes are as varied as one ought to expect of adult fish whose environment and habits can be so dissimilar.

Let us look at the different methods of spawning:

Egg Guardians There are a number of species that, far from ignoring the eggs once they are laid, actually gather and watch over them until they hatch, and then guard the youngsters — herding them into a place of safety in a manner reminiscent of sheepdogs. Members of the cichlid family are the best examples of this, including the ever-popular Angel fish, laying their eggs on the sides of flower pots, rocks, upright pieces of slate, or even thermo-

77

stat tubes: the parents having first hunted for a suitable site and then cleaned it carefully with their mouths for several days. The eggs are laid, and the parents take it in turns to 'fan' them with their fins, setting up a constant flow of water. When the eggs hatch, the fry will be transferred in the mouths of the parents to a safe spot — probably a shallow depression in the gravel — where they will remain until large enough to look after themselves. It is quite possible to breed some of the smaller species of Cichlid in a 3 ft. long community aquarium, providing there are no really aggressive fish present.

Egg Guardian 'fanning' eggs

Egg scatterers (non-adhesive eggs) The female chases up and down the aquarium, releasing a few eggs on each occasion: the male follows her closely, often nudging her, and as the eggs appear he fertilizes them. The eggs fall to the bottom of the aquarium, lying amongst the pebbles of a coarse grade of gravel: if the aquaruim were bare, the parents would come in search of the eggs once the spawning had been completed and hunger taken over. If the parents are now removed to another aquarium, the eggs will eventually hatch out — in one to three days for most species — and can be seen as small glass-like splinters hanging onto the sides of the aquarium. In a few more days the fry will start to swim about freely, usually gathering at the very top or very bottom of the aquarium. White Cloud Mountain Minnows and Zebra Danios are the most common, and easiest of the spawners in this group. It is possible to breed several pairs at the same time, providing they are all ready to spawn, otherwise the onlookers will merely eat the eggs, and it is good policy to include a small clump of plants such as Myriophylum or Elodea in which the female can rest if the male drives her too hard.

Egg scatterers (adhesive and semi-adhesive eggs) The pair will chase around the aquarium as a prelude to the actual spawning, which occurs in thickets of fine-leafed plants — Myriophyllum or Ambulia are ideal. Many of the eggs will adhere to the plants, but a layer of coarse gravel is again essential to help protect those that fall. Development follows the pattern described for the previous group. Barbs are typical of this spawning pattern, as are the Toothcarps (also known as 'Killifish') : in the case of this latter group, which are usually kept in small numbers with their own kind and are not generally accepted as 'community fish', they spawn in small artificial 'mops' made of nylon wool attached to corks, from which the eggs may be removed carefully by hand for hatching elsewhere. Eggs of no other fish will tolerate such handling.

Bubble-nest Builders Another type of fish that cares for its young is the Labyrinth fish, also known as an 'air breather' because of its ability to take gulps of air at the surface to supplement the oxygen extracted in the normal way through the gills ; this means that in the wild they can survive, for a time, in water that is so polluted that it could not support ordinary, non-labyrinth fishes. Their method of breeding is quite unusual, for they build a 'nest' of bubbles on the water surface — with some species it may be a full 3 in. in diameter and $\frac{1}{2}$ in. in height — into which they place the individual eggs as they are produced.

The spawning itself is fascinating to watch : the following description of a Siamese Fighter is typical of most of the labyrinths. Over a period of two or three days the male will construct the bubble-nest, sometimes including small pieces of floating plant. During this time the female will be kept well away, the male periodically chasing her or giving her a beautiful display of his finnage. When the nest is complete he will pay her more attention, courting her as a prelude to the spawning. The two will meet just

under the bubble nest, and the male will curve his body so as to embrace hers from underneath, squeezing her flanks until she releases some eggs : at the same moment he will fertilize them, and shortly afterwards relax his grip. By now the pair will have dropped nearly to the bottom of the aquarium, and the male will scurry around gathering up the eggs in his mouth and return to the nest, placing each egg in a separate bubble. When the female has recovered she will rejoin him at the surface, and the spawning sequence will continue until some 200-300 eggs have been laid. The male will then take charge, guarding and moving them around and blowing fresh bubbles as necessary, driving off the female (who should be carefully removed at this stage) and any other intruders. When the eggs hatch he will continue his guard duties, returning any stray fry to the safety of the bubbles. A further two or three days and they will be swimming strongly on their own ; and at this stage it is wise to remove the male before he decides to start eating his offspring.

Feeding the Fry
In the case of the livebearers, the young will take almost any finely powdered food, including what the parents are being given : in fact they rarely need any special attention in this respect, excepting species such as Half-beaks which will accept only live foods.

Egglayers need a series of different foods, each one tailored to the mouth size and appetite of the growing fry. For the first forty-eight hours they will be absorbing the yolk-sac on their bodies, and need no other food; when that is exhausted they require infusoria — microscopic aquatic creatures — or a proprietary liquid fry food which is an acceptable and more convenient substitute. It is difficult to assess exactly how much to give, but an average spawning of 150 young could be fed about ten drops every six or eight hours: the main thing is to keep their stomachs well filled, and this can be ascertained, after practice, with a powerful magnifying lens. At around fourteen days, progress to newly hatched brine shrimp or micro worms, in small quantities, and at the end of a further two or three weeks finely sifted daphnia and powdered dry foods may be given.

Diseases and ailments

Fish are susceptible to a wide range of ailments and troubles, but there are few that cannot be prevented or successfully treated if prompt action is taken. Many diseases are the direct or indirect result of incorrect care, and overcrowding is one of the worst offenders in this respect: other diseases occur as a result of the unwitting introduction of a parasite into an otherwise healthy aquarium. Although the hobbyist may go for years without encountering any such troubles, he should remember that proper identification and treatment is needed if the cure is to succeed.

Prevention is of course by far the best policy, and a quarantine tank quickly becomes an essential item for any serious fishkeeper; this tank should be quite bare, without rocks, gravel, or plants, and should be kept in readiness for any unexpected emergency. When new fish are purchased, they should be kept isolated in this quarantine tank for a period of not less than fourteen days: during this time any latent disease will develop, and can be treated accordingly. Once an infected fish is introduced into the main aquarium it will usually pass on its ailments to the other occupants: a complete cure then becomes that much more difficult and takes rather longer. In addition, some of the remedies, such as methylene blue, may have an injurious effect on the aquatic plants, so they should be used only in bare tanks except as a last resort. The fish may show signs that all is not well some time before the symptoms of a disease appear, and this will merit particular attention over the following days.

Such signs include lack of interest in food; fins closed up tightly against the body; fish that are usually active, hiding motionless in a corner; and fish repeatedly rubbing themselves against the rocks, plants, or gravel. In fact, any sudden change in the behaviour of the fish may be a prelude to something more serious.

Considering the main ailments that affect tropical fish, the beginner will certainly find it better to purchase a suitable remedy from a local aquatic supplier, accurately marked with correct dosage, rather than try to administer a home-made medicament whose effect and efficiency are uncertain.

FUNGUS AND FIN-ROT. These are bacterial diseases that are unlikely to occur in a well-kept aquarium where the fish are healthy, although occasionally a weak or injured specimen may contract one of them. Salt may be used as a remedy, but the author's favourite is Liquitox, a remedy widely available in Britain and America, and very effective if used as directed. If these troubles frequently recur, it is a sign that something is seriously amis in the conditions you provide for your fish.

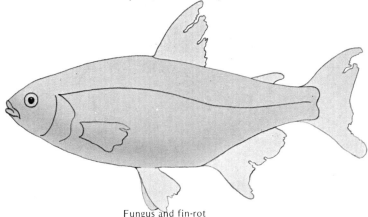

Fungus and fin-rot

WHITE SPOT. A parasitic disease, and one of the most common amongst tropical fish. Its presence is indicated by minute white dots, the size of a pin-prick, which appear initially in small numbers on the fins: if left untreated they will multiply and spread over the whole body until death ensues. A particularly contagious disease, it will affect almost all the occupants of the aquarium within a few days, and can be spread to other aquaria by means of wet hands, wet nets, or splashes, though it is usually introduced with newly purchased or newly imported fish.

A cure can be effected in one of two ways — by using a proprietary remedy or by raising the temperature. In the latter method the aquarium temperature is raised to 30-31 °C. until all the spots have disappeared: after a further four days lower the temperature to normal, and all should be well. Occasionally a disease of very similar appearance may be encountered, the spots being rather larger and more granular in form: in this case two rounded teaspoons of cooking salt per gallon of water should be added. As with all such medicaments, the salt should be thoroughly dissolved in a small quantity of water before being added to the aquarium. Once the disease has disappeared the salt concentration should be reduced by partial changes of the water, otherwise the plants may become affected.

VELVET. This has the appearance of a thin, matt, off-white coating, which covers almost the entire fish, fins included : by this time the fish will be looking a very sorry sight indeed, lying motionless in the water with the fins tightly closed. Livebearers seem to be particularly prone to this. Use either a proprietary remedy, or two rounded teaspoons of salt per gallon of water until a cure is achieved.

WASTING DISEASE. The fish becomes emaciated, losing the roundness and plumpness of its body, its sense of balance deteriorates, it becomes more sluggish, and its fins are closed up, often becoming ragged at the edges. These constitute what we might generally term a wasting disease, though it is more a collection of symptoms than a true disease. Very old fish will tend towards this state shortly before they die, but it can be found in quite young fish if they have been overcrowded and their growth stunted. 'Runts' — the term given to the weakest specimens in a particular brood — will often show similar signs. There is no real remedy other than prevention in the first place.

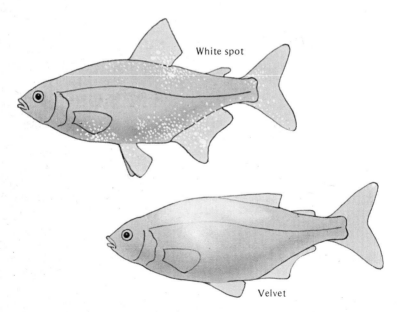

White spot

Velvet

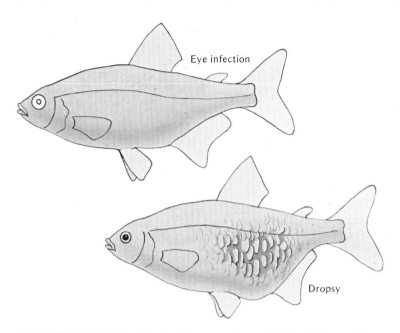

Eye infection

Dropsy

EYE INFECTIONS. Again, these are bacterial in origin, and may be the result of unsatisfactory conditions or actual damage. The surface of the eye should be quite transparent, and if it shows any sign of milkiness, or if it protrudes rather more than usual, an infection is probable. Liquitox seems to be a good remedy for this rather difficult trouble, and even if the sight in the eye is not saved it usually prevents the fish dying from a further spread of infection.

DROPSY. The fish becomes bloated, often being confused with one that is egg-bound, until the edges of the scales protrude from the fish — normally they lie quite flat except for those on certain members of the Panchax family. There appears to be no reliable cure, though unhealthy conditions do often seem to increase the incidence of the disease — another case of prevention being the answer.

SHIMMIES. This is when the fish remains motionless in mid-water, with its fins closed up, and 'wiggles' repeatedly. Sometimes it is an indication of a disease, but is often the result of a chilling of the fish when transporting it or moving it from tank to tank. A rise in temperature to 28-29 °C. will often effect a cure.

BOILS. Skin infections, such as boils, are usually a sign of unhealthy conditions in the aquarium, or occasionally that the particular fish is a poor specimen. Gouramies seem particularly susceptible to boils and the main action will be to prevent secondary infection by using Liquitox or a similar medicament against fungus. Tubifex worms are sometimes, and perhaps wrongly, blamed for causing boils.

SPLIT FINS. Your fish will occasionally show a split fin or two, and this is almost unavoidable: this is not always the result of a true fight, such as between cichlids, but is more often found with naturally playful fish, such as sharks and loaches, which chase each other harmlessly around the tank. These splits will heal up very rapidly, usually within a couple of days. If the damage is more extensive — such as chunks taken out of the fins — watch the occupants carefully to see if one is persistently bullying the others: but do not confuse this with the normal territorial guarding by some fish.

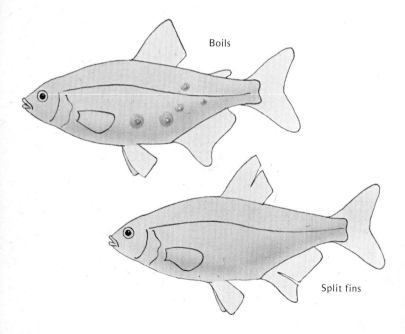

Boils

Split fins

POISONING. Ensure your fishkeeping equipment never comes into contact with soap, bleach, disinfectant, detergent, polish, and similar household products. Never use an aerosol fly spray or air freshner in a room with fish, and if any painting is to be done in the room cover the top of the aquarium with a blanket, switch off the aeration, and open the door and windows for as long as possible. Small quantities of rust from the aquarium frame will do no harm, but avoid any prolonged contact between copper, brass, zinc, or aluminium and the water, although small pieces of lead may safely be used to keep the plants weighted down.

EUTHANASIA. Eventually a fish may be so badly injured or infected that a cure is impossible : in such a case the kindest move would be to kill it as quickly and painlessly as possible. Flushing fish down the lavatory is neither of these things, for they can live many hours even in cold water. The best way is to tip the fish out of the net onto the ground out of doors, and hit it firmly with a brick or lump of stone : death this way is instantaneous, and can be carried out even by those who are squeamish about such things.

Although it might seem an odd idea, the fishkeeper should go out of his way to see and recognise the various diseases before they occur in his own aquaria, so that he can take the correct action in good time : a case of profiting by other people's misfortune. Just once in a while a fish will die suddenly and for no apparent reason, although its former companions remain in the best of health. These things happen everywhere in nature, and there is no need for self-recrimination, providing it remains just a rare event. If casualties among newly purchased fish become excessive, it may be time to find a new supplier : not all are as conscientious over quarantining and acclimatising their stock as we might like. Street markets should be avoided at all costs — the fish are cheap but have a very low chance of survival in inexperienced hands.

Where to from here?

By the time the reader has reached this point in the book, the chances are that the original plans for a modest aquarium have been superseded by more ambitious ones: if this is so, fruition of these ideas will naturally take some time. Once the number of tanks has reached double figures, however, the situation may call for reappraisal: are they dotted around the house, making routine servicing a chore? The time may well have come to group them in one place, in a 'fish-house' — a room or outside building devoted solely to fishkeeping. Such an arrangement will not only simplify work on the aquaria, but, providing the structure is suitably insulated against heat loss, can actually prove to be more economical.

Such a fish house would ideally be out-of-doors, with a concrete floor, so that spilled water runs away harmlessly. The roof should incorporate a double-glazed window equal to approximately one fifth of the floor area: the natural daylight that this admits suggests that few aquaria would need additional individual lighting. The inside of the walls and the remainder of the roof should be insulated with 2 in. of glass fibre, covered with hardboard, and given a final interior surface of $\frac{1}{2}$ in. expanded polystyrene. The door must be a snug fit so as to avoid draughts, and for preference should open into a further part of the shed or building rather than directly into the open. Provided these criteria are met, and they should be regarded as the minimum, such a fish-house need not be expensive to operate. In such circumstances the inside could be space-heated by tubular electrical greenhouse heaters or a small paraffin stove, obviating the need for individual heaters and thermostats in each aquarium. A fish-house about 6 ft. square, with a headroom of 6 ft. 6 in., can hold a considerable number of tanks if the staging is planned with some thought, and the potential of such an arrangement is almost limitless.

The time will come when some contact with other aquarists is desired. There are numerous societies fulfilling just such a rôle, some catering for a particular locality, others for individual types of fish. Membership of these societies is not expensive yet the benefits are enormous: most hold regular shows in addition to their usual meetings, and their ranks will probably include judges, lecturers, and specialists in all fields of the hobby.

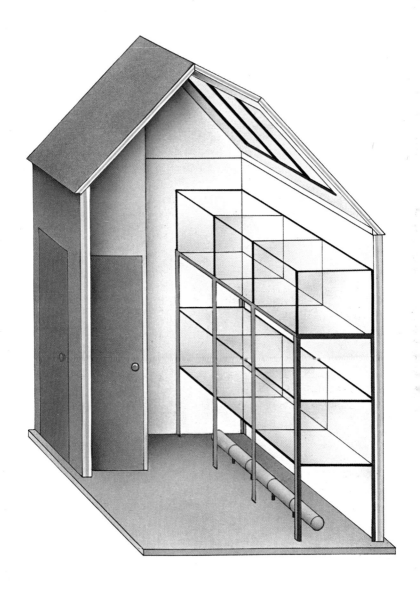

Cut-away shed suggesting a possible arrangement for a group of tanks

Useful information

In order to keep up to date on new products and all topics allied to the hobby, a subscription to an aquatic magazine can be an excellent investment. The principal ones in the English language are :

Petfish Monthly (P.F. Publications, 554 Garratt Lane, London S.W.17, England.)

The Aquarist & Pondkeeper (The Butts, Half Acre, Brentford, Middlesex, England.)

Tropical Fish Hobbyist (T.F.H. Publications Inc., 211 West Sylvania Ave., Neptune City, New Jersey, U.S.A.)

All three are widely available in the U.K. and the United States, and all publish details of societies, exhibitions, and other activities in addition to their normal editorial content.

Size of aquarium (in.)	Approx. water content (Imperial gallons)	(litres)	(lb.)	Surface area (in.²)
12 x 6 x 6	1½	6.75	15	72
14 x 8 x 8	3	13.5	30	112
16 x 8 x 8	4	18.0	40	128
18 x 10 x 10	6	27.0	60	180
24 x 12 x 12	12	54.0	120	288
24 x 12 x 15	15	67.5	150	288
30 x 12 x 15	20	90.0	200	360
36 x 12 x 15	23	103.5	230	432
48 x 15 x 15	40	180.0	400	720
72 x 15 x 18	70	315.0	700	1,080

Table courtesy of *P.F.M. Aquarist's Diary*

In practice, the actual water content of a set-up aquarium will generally be a little less than that shown : some will be displaced by the gravel and rockwork.

1 Imperial gallon of water weighs approx. 10lb.
1 U.S. gallon of water weighs approx. 8.3lb.
1 cubic foot of water weighs approx. 62.3lb.
1 cubic foot of water=approx. 6¼ Imperial gallons
(7½ U.S. gallons)

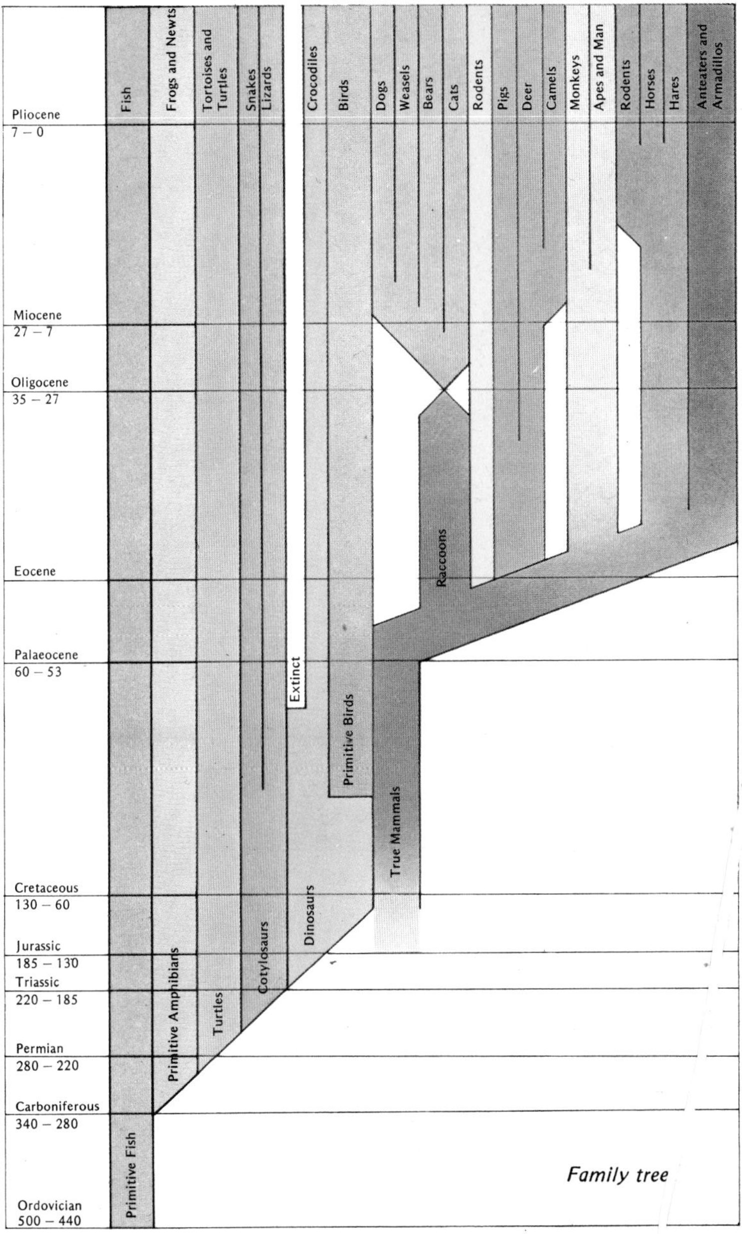
Pliocene
7 – 0
Miocene
27 – 7
Oligocene
35 – 27
Eocene
Palaeocene
60 – 53
Cretaceous
130 – 60
Jurassic
185 – 130
Triassic
220 – 185
Permian
280 – 220
Carboniferous
340 – 280
Ordovician
500 – 440
Fish
Frogs and Newts
Tortoises and Turtles
Snakes
Lizards
Crocodiles
Birds
Dogs
Weasels
Bears
Cats
Rodents
Pigs
Deer
Camels
Monkeys
Apes and Man
Rodents
Horses
Hares
Anteaters and Armadillos
Raccoons
Extinct
Primitive Birds
True Mammals
Dinosaurs
Cotylosaurs
Turtles
Primitive Amphibians
Primitive Fish

Family tree

Index